Words for a Dying World

Words for a Dying World

*Stories of Grief and Courage
from the Global Church*

Edited by Hannah Malcolm

scm press

© Editor and Contributors 2020

Published in 2020 by SCM Press
Editorial office
3rd Floor, Invicta House,
108–114 Golden Lane,
London EC1Y 0TG, UK
www.scmpress.co.uk

SCM Press is an imprint of Hymns Ancient & Modern Ltd
(a registered charity)

Hymns Ancient & Modern® is a registered trademark of
Hymns Ancient & Modern Ltd
13A Hellesdon Park Road, Norwich,
Norfolk NR6 5DR, UK

British Library Cataloguing in Publication data

A catalogue record for this book is available
from the British Library

978 0 334 05986 8

Typeset by Regent Typesetting
Printed and bound by
CPI Group (UK) Ltd

Contents

CONTENTS

Part 3: As It Will Be

This book is dedicated to
the people
the creatures
the earth
we have already sacrificed.

They were beloved too.

The majority of author royalties for this collection are split evenly between contributors. Half of those royalties have been pooled as a donation to Client Earth, who work globally to defend the rights of people and planet. The other royalties are directly supporting the contributors and communities represented here.

Contributors

Anderson Jeremiah

The Revd Dr Anderson H. M. Jeremiah is Lecturer of World
Christianity and Religious Studies in the department of Politics,
Philosophy and Religion at Lancaster University, UK. He is
an Anglican theologian and priest from the Church of South
India (an Anglican province). He currently serves the Church
of England in the Diocese of Blackburn, Lancashire. Anderson
is an elected member of the General Synod. His research interests and publications lie in the lived facet of world Christianity
and its theological and missional engagement with other faith
communities and the wider society. Anderson is also deeply
passionate about social justice as a gospel imperative and is
currently involved in a number of interreligious and peace
initiatives. Alongside being an expert in South Asian and West
African Christianity, he is also conducting research on diverse
ethnic and racial make-up and its implications for Christianity in
Britain. Anderson has published widely in the areas of contextual
theology, post-colonial theology, mission and ecumenical studies,
and culture and Christianity.

Anupama Ranawana

Anupama Ranawana is a writer and theologian based in Oxford.
Her work focuses primarily on feminist religious thought and
decolonial and critical race theory approaches to religion and
global politics.

Archuna Ananthamohan

Archuna Ananthamohan is a young poet, writer and film-maker. As a mental health campaigner, he frequently speaks at schools and other venues to raise awareness. He is the founder of ItMatters, a non-profit movement that explores mental health using the creative medium. Coming from a Hindu family but growing up in a Christian environment, faith has always played a pivotal role in his life. Archuna believes that Christ continues to inspire his poetry and writing, which he explores using Instagram. His mantra is 'to think critically, love radically; the Truth will set you free!'

Azariah France-Williams

Fr Azariah is a priest, poet and prophet, and ministers in the Diocese of Manchester. He is the author of *Ghost Ship: Institutional Racism and the Church of England*. Fr Azariah is really from Leeds in West Yorkshire. His accent has faded but there is a northern spirit at play. His parents were part of the Windrush generation, so as well as northern grit Fr Azariah has some sunshine in his heritage. As a dyslexic he sees the world a little differently to many and enjoys the power of words to animate and illuminate the world anew.

Bharadhydasan Kannan

Bharadhydasan Kannan has assisted research on marginalized communities like Dalits and Tribals of Tamil Nadu, covering their musicology and social life. He comes from a Hindu family and accepted the Lord Jesus at the age of 14. He works within church planting missions and welfare programmes. Being from an engineering background and witnessing the impact of development projects and industrialization on tribal groups, his focus shifted towards developing an inclusive and sustainable socio-economic growth model. He believes churches in India shy away from discussing 'identities' both within themselves and in the secular world. This includes displaced tribal groups, whose homelessness is hardly noticed or discussed in mainstream churches. Part of his work has been to initiate discussion among church groups and academic circles on loss of livelihood and the impact of industries on environment and human habitation.

Caleb Gordon

Caleb Gordon is a PhD student at the University of Manchester, writing and researching about theological treatments of aesthetic experience in environmental ethics. Though currently living in the UK, he is originally from Alaska, and Alaska continues to serve as a source of inspiration for his academic and creative projects. Prior to his PhD, Caleb balanced his winter studies by working on commercial fishing boats and on scientific projects for the Alaska Department of Fish and Game and the University of Alaska, Anchorage. These experiences both deepened his love for wilderness and prompted some of the difficult questions that stimulate his ongoing work.

Christopher Douglas-Huriwai

Christopher is a priest in the Anglican Church of Aotearoa, New Zealand, and Polynesia, currently serving as Canon to the Ordinary and Chaplain to the Archbishop. He is married to Sharlene and together they have a daughter, Te Aomihia. Christopher affiliates to the Ngati Porou, Ngai Te Rangi, Te Aitanga-a-Mahaki, Rongowhakaata, Raukawa and Maniapoto tribes, and has a passion for indigenous theology and liturgy. He is also on the staff of Te Rau Theological College, an indigenous theological college founded in 1882 and located on the east coast of the North Island where he teaches ministry formation and lectures in the areas of liturgics, cultural exegesis and indigenous theology.

David Benjamin Blower

David Benjamin Blower is a musician, writer and podcaster from Birmingham in the UK. In 2019 he released *We Really Existed and We Really Did This*, a record of reflections on ecological breakdown. He is part of Nomad Podcast, and has written several books, including *Sympathy for Jonah: Reflections on Terror, Humiliation and the Politics of Enemy-Love* (Resource Publications, 2016).

Debo Oluwatuminu

Debo is a poet, writer, director, facilitator, collaborator and producer who conceives, writes and collaborates with creatives in the fields of theatre, film and TV to produce what he calls 'heart-transforming art'. He is dedicated to finding fresh ways to illustrate how to 'live' the Christian message in the world today. He has worked in Israel with Palestinians and Israelis on the British Mandate, which he explored from a Christian perspective. He was the Head writer, script editor and creative consultant on EbonyLife TV's adaptation of Season One of the popular ABC/Disney series *Desperate Housewives*, called *Desperate Housewives Africa*, among other projects. He is also involved in the Christian Aid Worship and Theology group, and works with theologians, creatives and academics to create prayer and worship resources for their partners around the world. He serves as the Chair of Trustees in his local church and occasionally preaches and teaches God's word. Debo has an MA in writing for performance from Goldsmiths University, London, and an MLitt from St Andrews University, Scotland, in 'The Bible and the Contemporary World'. He is a strong believer in making the values and principles of the kingdom practically relevant both in the 'Church' and within contemporary culture. He is associated with the Institute of the Imagination, Theatre and the Arts (IITA), and the African Theatre Association (AfTA), based at Goldsmiths College, London.

Debra Murphy

Debra Dean Murphy is Associate Professor of Religious Studies at West Virginia Wesleyan College. She is the author of *Teaching that Transforms: Worship as the Heart of Christian Education* (Wipf & Stock, 2006), *Happiness, Health, and Beauty: The Christian Life in Everyday Terms* (Cascade Books, 2015), and numerous articles, essays, and book reviews. She is a featured columnist for *The Christian Century*, where her subject matter has included prayer, poetry, climate collapse, restorative justice, and the teaching life. She is Roman Catholic and a member of the Catholic Committee of Appalachia. Debra also serves on the board of directors of the Ekklesia Project, an ecumenical network of Christians and Christian communities committed to the non-violent way of Jesus.

Dianne Rayson

Di Rayson is an adjunct research fellow in the Public and Contextual Theology Research Centre at Charles Sturt University, Australia. She is a public theologian who researches ecotheology and ecoethics, influenced by the life and work of Dietrich Bonhoeffer. She lectures at several universities and has published on war and ecology, rape culture, Bonhoeffer and Gandhi, and 'earthly Christianity'. She has had former careers in community development and public health, working in Papua New Guinea and Australia's Northern Territory. Di lives on a small farm in Biripi country, surrounded by forests and mountains and not too far from the ocean. Her forthcoming book with Lexington Press is titled *Bonhoeffer and Climate Change: Theology and Ethics*.

Elia Maggang

Elia Maggang lives in Kupang City, West Timor, Indonesia. Elia spent his childhood in the coastal areas (Pasir Panjang and Nunbaun Delha) of the city. Swimming in the sea, playing football on the beach, fishing from the shorelines and collecting seafood during low tide with his friends were the daily activities that made him love the sea so much. That experience also helped him to understand the significance of the sea for the poor people and artisanal fishers, and the severe impacts of climate change for the sea and those people. Many of his childhood friends and former neighbours are dependent on the sea for their food and livelihood. Elia is currently writing a PhD on a theological approach to sea conservation in Indonesia. He is a member of Gereja Masehi Injili di Timor (the Protestant Evangelical Church in Timor).

Emma Lietz Bilecky

Emma Lietz Bilecky is currently a fellow at Princeton Theological Seminary's Farminary. She has an abiding interest in land and seeks to understand how people, landscapes and words about God shape one another. She holds a Master of Theological Studies from Duke Divinity School and a Master of Environmental Management from the Nicholas School of the Environment, where she studied food systems, environmental policy and land loss. She works to heal the personal, collective and ecological wounds of settler colonial Christianity while building soil.

Grace Thomas

Grace Thomas originally graduated with a degree in nursing and gained an MA in Healthcare Ethics and Law, both from the University of Manchester, UK. She spent time as a researcher, publishing papers in women's sexual health and scar conditions that predominantly affect black and brown people, before responding to a call for ordination in the Church of England. During her ordination training, as part of an MA in theology at Chester University, Grace undertook research into female clergy well-being, and developed a tool that is now in use by clergy in Manchester Diocese and beyond. Grace is currently serving her curacy in Manchester, and teaches pastoral care and theological reflection in two local theological colleges. Her interests remain in the fields of well-being, feminist theology, the Church's response to the climate crisis, diversity and inclusion, and how these different issues intersect. Grace is an active member of Christian Climate Action and, in the Christmas of 2019, she wrote some climate carols that were sung by groups in the UK and around the world.

Hannah Malcolm

Hannah is training to be a priest in the Church of England and writing a PhD on theology and climate and ecological grief. She is a member of Christian Climate Action and set up their regional Manchester group. She regularly speaks on the Church and climate, and has previously written for Theos Think Tank, *Church Times*, Radio 4's 'Thought for the Day', and Christian Climate Action's *Time to Act*, edited by Jeremy Williams.

Holly-Anna Petersen

Holly-Anna Petersen has a degree in biology, a masters in psychology and a Postgraduate Certificate in LI Cognitive Behavioural Interventions. She works as a mental health practitioner in the NHS, treating people with a range of emotional difficulties. Holly is a trustee of Operation Noah, a charity that campaigns on church fossil fuel divestment. She is also a founding member of Christian Climate Action, a non-violent direct action group, which works alongside others in the movement, such as Extinction Rebellion and Phulbari Solidarity.

Hugh Jones

Hugh Jones is a parish priest in the City and Diocese of Lincoln where he also serves as Rural Dean and is a Priest Vicar at Lincoln

Cathedral. He teaches philosophy of religion at Bishop Grosse-
teste University. Prior to ordination, Hugh studied psychology to
doctoral level before joining the home civil service. After a long
illness forced him to take early retirement, he developed a free-
lance career as a musician, music teacher and technical author.
He trained for ordination at Ripon College Cuddesdon and was
ordained in the Diocese of Lincoln in 2010. He served his title
in Boston before becoming Vicar of St Nicholas Church in 2014.
He is married with two grown-up sons.

Isabel Mukonyora

Isabel Mukonyora is an international scholar of religion whose
training began with an undergraduate degree in theology, followed by a Master of Letters degree in the history of religions
from the University of Aberdeen in Scotland and a Doctor of
Philosophy Degree from the Faculty of Theology at Oxford
University, UK. She has been teaching at Western Kentucky University since 2014 and is now a full professor.

Jione Havea

Jione Havea is a native pastor (Methodist Church in Tonga) and
research fellow in religious studies with Trinity Methodist Theological College (Auckland, Aotearoa New Zealand) and with the
Public and Contextual Theology research centre (Charles Sturt
University, Australia).

Jon Seals

Jon Seals is a conceptual artist, teacher and curator. He holds
an MAR from Yale Divinity School and Yale Institute of Sacred
Music, and an MFA in Painting from Savannah College of Art
and Design. His artistic practice is organized around exploring
the ways in which identity relates to memory, loss and redemp-

tion in visual culture. He is Associate Professor and Chair of the Department of Art and Digital Media at Olivet Nazarene University.

Julia Kendal

Julia Kendal is a storyteller and social justice advocate. She has spent the last ten years engaging and supporting people in making choices that are good for all of creation – people and planet. She currently works for the international development charity Tearfund, advocating on global issues such as climate change and waste. Julia is a poet and a writer, with a regular column in *Clarity* magazine. She shares about her own sustainable living journey at *Papier-mâché Thoughts*. She is regularly called away from her laptop by the sound of a pager as volunteer lifeboat crew with the Royal National Lifeboat Institution (RNLI) on the River Thames. You can read more of her writing at https://papier machethoughts.com or find her on Twitter at @JuliaRKendal.

Kyle Lambelet

Dr Kyle Lambelet is Assistant Professor in the Practice of Theology and Ethics at Emory University's Candler School of Theology. He teaches and researches at the intersection of political theology, religious ethics and social change. His first book, *¡Presente! Nonviolent Politics and the Resurrection of the Dead* (Georgetown University Press, 2019), explores the moral and political dimensions of non-violent struggle through an extended case study of the movement to close the School of the Americas. His current research examines the apocalyptic dimensions of talk and action around climate change, and how apocalyptic political theologies can offer resources for pastoral and political engagement in the midst of endings. Lambelet worked for several years in faith-rooted organizing for racial and economic justice in the south-east United States. He lived for a season at the Open Door Community, a Catholic Worker community in Atlanta, and worked with the Greensboro Truth and Community Reconciliation project, the first citizen-initiated truth and reconciliation process in the United States. He continued his education with an MTS at Vanderbilt University Divinity School and a PhD in the joint degree programme in Theology and Peace Studies at the University of Notre Dame.

Leigh Kern

Leigh Kern is a printmaker, musician, artist, priest and prison chaplain based in Toronto and the current territories of the Anishnawbe Nation and Haudenosaunee Confederacy. The cover art of this book is titled 'Our love is like mountains' and was created in support of the protectors of Mauna Kea. The second block print featured in this publication is titled 'Offering'. Kern's work is based on ritual, community, contemplation and action.

Maggi Dawn

The Revd Professor Maggi Dawn (MA, PhD, Cantab) is a songwriter, theologian and author. She is currently Professor of Theology at Durham University (UK), having previously taught at Yale University (USA) and the University of Cambridge (UK). Her first career was in the music business, as a singer, musician and songwriter, and she later turned these gifts to writing hymns and songs for Christian worship.

María Alejandra Andrade Vinueza

María Alejandra Andrade Vinueza is an Ecuadorian sociologist and theologian, with interest in issues related to faith, spirituality, decoloniality and justice. She works for Tearfund as the Theology and Network Engagement Lead, promoting global theological thinking and supporting the mobilization of Christian communities to alleviate poverty, stop the degradation of the environment and promote justice. She has the privilege of dis-covering life together with her husband, Frank, and with her two children, José and Mati.

Nangula Eva-Liisa Kathindi

My name is Nangula Eva-Liisa Kathindi, an Anglican Priest in the Diocese of Namibia. I live in Oshakati, northern Namibia. My experience includes working among church youth after I had finished my studies in sociology and theology in the United States of America. When Namibians were preparing to receive those who were in exile for the purpose of liberating the country, I mobilized church women to prepare the reception of returnees from exile in 1989. I am one of the first two women who were ordained priests in the Anglican Diocese of Namibia in 1994. In 1997 I served as parish priest. I served as a member of the Central Committee of the World Council of Churches for two separate terms of seven years (1991–8 and 2006–13), represent-ing the Anglican Church of Southern Africa. Between 1999 and 2005 I served as first woman General Secretary of the Council of Churches in Namibia. In 2006 I was appointed first woman Dean of St George's Cathedral in Windhoek. From 2007 to 2008 I served as Provincial Executive Officer of the Archbishop of Cape Town in Cape Town, RSA. From 2011 to 2017 I served as first woman Chief Chaplain of the Namibian Defence Force. Currently I supervise six parishes in northern Namibia and coordinate a Diocesan School for Ministries, guiding people to discern their vocation to ministry.

Oana Marian

Oana Sanziana Marian is a Romanian-born, US-raised artist and writer currently pursuing a PhD in theology from Trinity College, Dublin. She is a co-founder of the Active Hope Network, a com-munity that aims to bridge political activism, spirituality and collective thriving.

Panu Pihkala

Dr Panu Pihkala is an expert in eco-anxiety and Lutheran Pastor. He researches the subject in the University of Helsinki, leads practical workshops on the theme, develops educational materials, and writes popular books. Pihkala is an adjunct professor (Title of Docent) of environmental theology in the Faculty of Theology at the University of Helsinki and a postdoctoral researcher in the HELSUS Sustainability Science Institute. Pihkala's dissertation (2014) rediscovered various forms of Christian ecotheology from the first half of the twentieth century, including theological work from the British Isles. Currently, Pihkala is the leading Finnish expert in interdisciplinary research about eco-anxiety and climate anxiety. Pihkala's pioneering monograph on the subject ('Päin helvettiä? Ympäristöahdistus ja toivo – Eco-anxiety and Hope') was published in Finnish in October 2017 and has raised much public discussion in Finland. Pihkala's latest book is a 300-page popular handbook of 'ecological emotions' (*Mieli maassa? Ympäristötunteet*). Pihkala has been an active public intellectual in Finland, giving over 50 interviews a year during the last years. He often co-operates with artists and educators. Pihkala was awarded the National Prize for Adult Education (Sivistyspalkinto) in 2018 by the Finnish Lifelong Learning Foundation (Kansanvalistusseura) for his work related to eco-anxiety.

Peter Fox and Miles Giljam

Peter Fox and Miles Giljam live in Cape Town, South Africa. Peter is a minister with the Uniting Presbyterian Church; a grief counsellor and author. Miles Giljam works in Public Affairs for Tearfund and SACLI. Their chapter is written in their personal capacities.

Pilar Vicentelo Euribe

Pilar is an agronomist engineer, who graduated from the National Agrarian University, La Molina, with more than 20 years of trajectory linked to sustainable development processes from small agriculture and educational institutions. Her work has been linked mainly to different organizations for civil society, as well as national and international networks for climate change. Currently, she is head of the Christian development organization Vida Abundante, which has more than ten years of experience and has won the first Environmental National Prize, given in the context of the COP 20.

Seoyoung Kim

Seoyoung Kim is a PhD student supervised by Professor Peter Scott at the University of Manchester, UK. Her research focuses on a theology of water in response to the context of a global water crisis. Seoyoung is an ordained minister of the Presbyterian Church in the Republic of Korea (PROK).

Sophia Chirongoma

Sophia is an African woman who is passionate about writing and publishing on the interconnections between earth justice and the current ecological crisis bedevilling the subaltern in the Third World with special reference to her home country, Zimbabwe. Although she is a Christian and draws most of her theological reflections from the Bible and Christian tradition, some of her theological resources are drawn from the African indigenous knowledge systems and traditions, particularly the Karanga-Shona world view in Zimbabwe, which is her cultural heritage. Currently, she is serving as a senior lecturer in the Religious Studies Department at Midlands State University, Zimbabwe. She is also an Academic Associate/Research Fellow at the Research Institute for Theology and Religion (RITR) in the College of Human Sciences, University of South Africa (UNISA).

Tim Gordon

Tim Gordon is a marine biologist at the University of Exeter and the Australian Institute of Marine Science. His research focuses on the impacts of climate change on tropical coral reefs. Working on Australia's Great Barrier Reef, he has recorded some of the most severe environmental destruction in human history, but still aims to find ways to protect marine life and all that it provides for people. He regularly discusses his work in schools, churches, conferences and the media, with audiences ranging from primary school children to prime ministers. He believes that combining science and faith can help us marvel at the natural world and learn to live sustainably as part of creation. In 2018, Tim was named the Society of Experimental Biology's Young Scientist of the Year.

Tim Middleton

Tim Middleton first trained as a scientist, completing a PhD in earth sciences at the University of Oxford. His scientific work examined earthquakes at the margins of the Ordos Plateau in northern China, and he was previously a stipendiary lecturer in earth sciences at St Anne's College, Oxford. Currently, Tim is a doctoral student in theology – also in Oxford – where his research focuses on intersections between ecotheology, trauma studies and contemporary philosophy. He is especially interested in how the category of trauma, and our theological responses to it, might help us to register the severity of contemporary ecological devastation. Within Oxford, Tim is a member of both the Laudato Si' Research Institute and an interdisciplinary network that is investigating climate crisis thinking in the humanities and social sciences. He also sits on the editorial board of the *Journal of the Oxford Graduate Theological Society*. Since 2018, Tim has been the Communications Officer at the William Temple Foundation – a think tank working on the role of religion and belief in public life. He is also an Associate of the Faraday Institute of Science and Religion and regularly leads workshops in schools as part of the God and the Big Bang project.

Victoria Marie

Victoria Marie is an African American/Canadian woman, priest, poet, indigenous rights and climate justice advocate, and author of *Transforming Addiction: The Role of Spirituality in Learning Recovery from Addictions.* She serves the Our Lady of Guadalupe Tonantzin faith community in Vancouver, which practises a renewed and inclusive Roman Catholic tradition where all are welcome. On 18 May 2018, she was arrested and sentenced to 120 hours' community service for violating the injunction against peaceful protest within five metres of the Kinder Morgan Tank Farm on Burnaby Mountain, currently the Trans Mountain Tank Farm. Unintimidated, on the second Saturday of every month, she joins an interdenominational group on Burnaby Mountain to pray for climate justice, especially the cessation of pipeline construction for transporting fossil fuels. See http://victoria-marie. blogspot.com.

Preface

This is an incomplete book. There are many places, peoples and griefs that are not recorded here, and the balance of contributors is not reflective of either global populations or where this grief falls hardest. This is as much a result of my own limitations as it is the product of publishing in the UK, in English, in a finite amount of time. And, of course, it is a product of the bleak reality that a book representing the grief of the Church over the whole world could never be completed, would never be big enough. That is a work that belongs to all of us, and this is my first step.

The process of gathering the following stories emerged out of my desire to see a shift in the dominant theological approaches to climate change and ecological collapse. Our churches are becoming increasingly adept at proposing good things Christians should do in response to these crises: personal and structural changes to energy use, signing petitions, 'nature' spirituality, and so on – all are worthy of our time and attention. But perhaps out of guilt or fear we still struggle to articulate what it means to acknowledge that which is already lost, and that which it is too late to save. Our failure to acknowledge these things does not make them go away. The blood of our siblings still cries out from the ground. I am of the belief that unless we find the courage to uplift voices of grief and anger both within the Church and without, we will continue to fall short of our call to participate in God's reconciling work. Reconciliation will begin in truly understanding its necessity; its backdrop of irrevocable loss.

This is my first attempt at editing a collection, and I naively decided that we would put the whole thing together in a little over a year. When those discussions began in 2019, there was no pandemic, no serious push for 'green recovery' plans from governments or corporations, and nowhere near the same far-reaching support for the Black Lives Matter movement. Somehow this project has emerged in 2020 anyway, perhaps in part because changing our narratives concerning climate and local ecologies feels more urgent than ever. I am immensely grateful to everyone who trusted me with their stories, graciously received my edits and suggestions, and offered contributions even in the midst of so much unexpected turmoil and trauma across the globe. Many of the stories and essays within this collection speak to immense courage, and no small part of that courage has been in the willingness to share them here.

As you read, you'll discover a range of different approaches, perspectives and styles. It includes people who write for a living and people who are being published for the first time. It includes poetry and song, eye-witness accounts, readings of Scripture, the experience of activists, and the histories of people and places. So, I offer you an incomplete book. Its beauty is at least in part by virtue of its incompleteness. My hope is that it both wounds and heals. My hope is that you feel invited to participate in a much wider conversation about what it means to express Christian faith in a time of loss – even the loss of the world itself. My hope is that you will both agree and disagree with its contents, and that you will be provoked to ask searching questions about your own grief, or perhaps the lack of it. Finally, my hope is that you will be provoked into solidarity, and that you might find the courage to answer the call of God to the people of God in the days ahead.

Introduction:
The End of the World?

Depending on who you ask, the world began to end 10 years ago, or 50 years ago, or 250 years ago, or 400 years ago.

Depending on who you ask.

Some have described this world-ending as the 'Anthropocene', a term defining a new geological epoch, dominated by human influence on climate and ecosystems. The precise beginning of the Anthropocene (and the ending of the 'natural' world) is up for debate. Was it the early seventeenth century, when European settlers killed so many Native Americans that global carbon dioxide levels hit a sudden low? Was it the Industrial Revolution, propelled by the labour of slaves, and super-charging our greenhouse fate? Perhaps it is signified by our mega predatory slaughter of other species, and the frightening acceleration of those institutions over the last 50 years. Philosopher Timothy Morton will tell you that the end of the world is an event that has already occurred twice; first in April 1784, with the invention of the steam engine, and again in 1945 when the first atom bomb was tested.[1] Perhaps it is still ahead of us – don't the headlines say we have ten years left?

This is a book about our relationships to these endings: what they signify, and how we talk about them.

The last ten years has seen a sudden and rapidly growing interest in naming our experiences of climate breakdown, ecological collapse and animal extinction. There has been an explosion in the number of people reporting grief, anxiety and traumatic

---

1 Timothy Morton, 2013, *Hyperobjects: Philosophy and Ecology after the End of the World*, Minneapolis, MN: University of Minnesota Press.

stress as a result of increased extreme weather events, the loss of flora and fauna, or a growing awareness of the existential threat that climate breakdown represents. These responses have been given various names, including but not limited to *solastalgia*, *tierratrauma*,[2] environmental melancholia,[3] and climate or ecological grief, mourning and anxiety. The diversity of terminology reflects the complexity of what we try to name. We are navigating the relationship between two constantly shifting concepts – human nature and non-human nature – and attempting to articulate a great trauma, where that relationship does not simply shift, but ruptures, breaks, disintegrates. And descriptions of this trauma have only recently emerged in English, though they have a longer human history. Still, we try to talk about it. Of course, we must. But attempts to describe this relationship in light of climate and ecological breakdown tend either to romanticize the non-human ('we need to learn from Mother Nature'), flatten the obvious differences between humans and other creatures in order to emphasize similarities ('we are nature defending itself'), or demonize all human activity ('humans are the virus'). These approaches aren't necessarily all equally damaging, but they do share a common problem: they expand personal or cultural interpretations of the relationship between humans and other creatures into universal and universalizing claims: Mother Nature is comfortably claimed as a teacher when we do not live in fear of smallpox. We say that we are 'nature defending itself' to decry littering while also promoting the nature-transcending ethics of veganism. And it is very easy to claim that 'humans are the virus' when no one is threatening to wipe out your particular group. Our grief about a dying world – however all-consuming it might feel – is not about death in abstraction. We grieve the death of particular things, whether creatures or places, and, until we understand this, our relationship between others and ourselves, we will continue to flounder in slogans and simplifications.

---

2 Glenn Albrecht, 2019, *Earth Emotions: New Words for a New World*, Ithaca, NY: Cornell University Press.

3 Renee Lertzman, 2016, *Environmental Melancholia: Psychoanalytic Dimensions of Engagement*, Abingdon: Routledge.

To put it another way: if grief is an expression of love, our grief takes on the shape of the places and creatures to whom we intimately belong. We mourn the death of the world because it is where we come from. But we do not come from the same places. We cannot emphasize our creatureliness without understanding our locality. We are finite, belonging to a particular community, and that finitude is not a barrier to our flourishing, but a gift. When we talk about a dying world – a whole biosphere diminishing in its stability and diversity – we are not describing a homogenous death event. Our sites of loss are particular – creatures, seasons and rhythms, futures, forests *that we know.* And grief is always expressed by particular individuals. It is to the loss of the particular that this book turns. And turning to the particular reveals that the weight of death has fallen unevenly. To say that all humans are and will be wounded by these losses is not equivalent to saying that all humans are wounded in the same way or to the same extent. If the sources of grief are diverse, our attempts to express it should be no less rooted in the variegated meanings of our contexts and experiences. And so any theological assessment of a dying world must likewise anticipate the myriad sources and expressions of climate and ecological grief.

But we must be wary. Grief is not only or always an expression of love but can also be wielded as power. We are beginning to acknowledge that the grief of some humans is heard, makes headlines and provokes response more readily than others – but we have yet to fully appreciate the ways power also manifests in the *content* of the grief itself. For example, despairing language about climate collapse in the minority world often reflects a kind of hubris: this despair rests on the assumption that the future is known and nothing can be done. The dominant culture I inhabit is a post-colonial one, founded on the assumption of a superior capacity for rule, seized through violence against land and people. In the West, we have imagined ourselves as the great problem-solvers and architects of the earth. Perhaps we are now pricked by guilt at the cost of our position, but we still assume that our position is the one from which improvement, or even salvation, will emerge – that is, if it is to emerge at all. It should not surprise us that when we fail to prevent the continued assault on our fellow creatures, we struggle to imagine that an alternative other than destruction is possible. The growing dominance of despair narratives is a warning to us that our grief both reflects our power and wields it. As I sit in the heart of global wealth accumulation, I can choose to express grief as the resigned acceptance of what I assume is inevitable, and yet rest assured that I am not and will not be the first to die in our morbid apocalyptic fantasies.

The orientation and content of our grief is a moral problem. If grief can wield dangerous power, it is not good enough to treat all of our feelings as simply rooted in our 'natural' relationship to the rest of creation, and therefore innately worthy of expression. The question of who grieves, and how, and what, is potent. If a particular and minority perspective continues to perform climate or ecological grief in ways that treat it as ultimate, or universal, we will begin to believe that *our version of grief* can be trusted as *innately and universally true*. That is the route to despair. And despair – especially when it is deliberately inculcated in others – is selfish, and cruel. Grief should be neither of those things.

I began this project with the conviction that rooting a theological response to climate grief in particular places really mattered. But what has emerged are stories that emphasize that this grief not only belongs in place, but in time. These are not just grief locations – spontaneous eruptions of sorrow from a wounded earth – but grief histories. The earth remembers, even when the people have forgotten. Perhaps that is what is really meant by an Anthropocene; a period in time when the earth can no longer forget our deeds. 'As far as the East is from the West, so far has God removed our sins from us', the Psalmist promised. But what if our sin has infiltrated every corner of the earth? Where will our sins go now? This book tries to reflect that spatial-temporal reality – we offer you portraits of grief from six continents, roughly split into three 'times'. The divisions are not intended as definitive, either in summarizing the themes explored in each piece, or in prescribing the order you should read them. But they do represent a rough flow: from the places and people we've been, to the groaning of the world around us, to the futures – longed for or imagined with dread – that await us. As you read, you'll find that these categories of time and space repeatedly break down, question each other, wrestle for attention: many of us no longer belong to just one place, sometimes through choice and increasingly through necessity. We are forced to bear the griefs of multiple places. Histories clash and compete. And grief over a dying world also disorients allegiance to a particular present: grieving for a history you are forced to carry and grieving for a future that may or may not come to pass.

Nevertheless, our grief belongs to times and places, and this is how we will begin to understand what it means to lose the whole: piece by piece. This book also begins from the assumption that particular experiences and universal claims about reality are not mutually exclusive. The ways we talk about our particular lives in a dying world do not encompass truth in their own right, but they can and should point to it. And so the language the Church uses to describe this grief matters; more is demanded of us than simply trying to mitigate the damage already done. We can begin to understand the universal task we have been given by listening to the particular members of the body of Christ. This is not a new idea. In fact, it is an ancient one. The Spirit does not belong to just a few of us, and the Church discerns her role by listening to herself, and most importantly by listening to her members who have been trampled on, silenced or abused. If we are to practise our grief in ways that are healing, rather than destructive, we will need to learn how. The book you hold invites you to begin this work.

Honouring grief does not mean honouring suffering – those who live under the constant and contemporary trauma of ecological collapse do not get to opt in or out of this vulnerability. Saying that grief can be good and holy is not the same as saying that suffering is good and holy, or that more reasons to grieve leads to more sanctification. But if the body of Christ is to orient ourselves to grief, then we must begin by hearing and defending those who have no choice in the matter. And if we are to interpret this grief as the vocation of the body of Christ, we must understand it not as an unbidden or spontaneous reflex, but as learned behaviour: even more than that, grief is a stance that the Church must learn to adopt in relation to the whole world, with each member oriented to the part they have been given. The embrace of grief as an ecclesial calling does not mean that we should only feel sadness, or that sorrow is more holy than joy. But it affirms that we are disciples of 'the man of sorrows, well acquainted with grief'. Let us listen to our teacher. If and when we do, I am convinced we will find that our grief can be powerful, not to oppress but to heal. When we choose a grief orientation that properly reflects our finitude as creatures, we participate in God's orientation towards the earth – the One who takes on flesh to dwell among flesh, in time and space, and tastes death. This changes our nature and changes the nature of the things we grieve. They become to us what they already are to God: beloved.

The essays and stories that follow offer some proposals for how the body of Christ might talk about these beloved things at the end of the world: here is what we have lost. Here is how we have suffered. Here is how we have sinned. The writers in this book share my conviction that life emerges from death: if one world is ending, God will continue to breathe life. But that does not mean that the end is only imagined. The truth is, it could have been different. And the knowledge of what we might have done – *should have done* – is sufficient cause to grieve, even if we have begun the work of repentance. The Son is reconciling all creation to himself because he became Jesus of Nazareth – born to a particular family, friends with particular people, living alongside particular creatures. We follow him in a willingness to love the times and places we have been given, even as we prepare to lose them.

To see the dying as beloved requires courage and is a calling we often try to avoid. As the numbered dead grow, they become overwhelming to the point of meaningless. Statistical descriptions of our fellow creatures as objects and investments hardens us against their loss. We talk about overpopulation and resource scarcity so that we can imagine human lives as competing goods and feel relieved when it is our life that is protected. We sanitize the bloody intimacy of famine and conflict with talk of politics and economics and regulations. But being willing to accept that the dying are beloved – and to treat them as beloved, even when we cannot save them – will soften us. It will make us vulnerable. The tenderness of caring for the dying is not a despairing act but a courageous one. It insists on the goodness of the body even when it seems that the body has nothing left to give. Adopting an orientation of grief means choosing to invest in things that are small, that are temporary, and celebrating them in the broken, fragile beauty they bear in the eyes of God. It is soft, cruciform foolishness. I hope that reading this book softens you. It has softened me.

PART I

As It Was Then

I

Overdue

JULIA KENDAL

Keep your words.
Stuff them
down the back of your throat
where I have learned to swallow mine.

scraped raw, but
never quite deep
enough to spit them out

You caught
the last five minutes
of the radio,
television,
found an article in a
tattered corner of the internet,

echo back at me
the words I've been struggling
to digest for years,
as if this is my first taste

stomach churns
on shadows
that never set

chatter through calamity
while someone passes the salt.

Display the speck of dirt under your nails;
pristine oblivion
that too closely mirrors my own

ears drown
in my own screams;
full to yours

I offer only silence;
maybe because it's all I received,
that or
a polite nod
that recognized truth
but left it standing at the door.

So this is a self-taught
tightrope walk,
rigid to the rules,
broken in the moment –

Gracelessly falling;
how can I offer
what I never gave myself?

clattering;
golden mean missed
again

Wasn't this what I wanted?
To be met
in the conversation;
but I've long slipped from my seat

I tried years ago;

now feels too late.

Theology unapplied

It looks like we're not the outliers any more. In recent years, much of the world has turned its gaze to this climate emergency. Now the family member who seemed to close their ears is the first to raise it over the dinner table. That meat-loving friend is an evangelist for vegetarianism (and not just for the health benefits). This, surely, is the moment that we earlier adopters were striving for.

But its arrival has come with a new form of grief. Because it feels like it has come too late. For the world, yes, as 1.5 degrees seems like an ever-fading dream. But also for ourselves.

What did we want for all those years? Camaraderie, I think. A sense of figuring out this journey in community. Try, learn, grieve, fail, forgive. Ourselves more often than not.

Because it is not easy to keep walking a path lined with the inevitability of mistakes. All have, and do, fall short. Climate-conscious living is no different. In this frightening new world I have found myself turning to an ancient way: the golden mean of Aristotle and Thomas Aquinas. A route of balance between apparent extremes, 'a middle way ... between a wholesale immersion in consumer culture and an unrelenting abandonment', as theologian Ruth Valerio puts it.[1] The golden mean acknowledges that our low-carbon lives will be imperfect; we will fall, to one extreme or the other. In encouraging us to keep seeking the central path, it offers grace for the moments when we don't. This empowers us to carry on.

If, that is, we receive that grace.

I find myself thinking of the Samaritan woman who met Jesus at the well.[2] She had sinned and been sinned against (it was men who had the power over women to take, divorce, leave). She is often portrayed as unfaithful, but society had not been faithful to her.[3] Let down, she lived on the margins, fetching water in the

---

1 Ruth Valerio, 2016, *Just Living: Faith and Community in an Age of Consumerism*, London: Hodder and Stoughton.

2 John 4.

3 Stephen Moyter, 1995, 'Jesus and the Marginalised in the Fourth Gospel', in Anthony Billington, Tony Lane and Max Turner (eds), *Mission and Meaning: Essays Presented to Peter Cotterell*, Carlisle: Paternoster, pp. 70–89.

heat of midday. And there she encounters Jesus, who offers living water 'to whoever drinks'. His grace is there for the taking.

The woman doesn't just drink; she hurries to invite others to 'Come, see a man who told me everything I've ever done. Could this be the Messiah?' (John 4.29, NIV). She is generous with her encounter. And I wonder if, in asking her neighbours this question, she too sought to figure things out in community. Where sin separates, grace unifies. When we accept it.

With this poem, I sought to capture what happens when we don't. It is, in a sense, theology unapplied. In the face of perceived apathy, I became more rigid to the rules that I'd made. Feeling forsaken by others, I became hard-hearted to myself. And now many more people are trooping this way. And instead of being enthused, I am indifferent. Built for community, my gracelessness further isolates.

This is not a path. It is a spiral, down. Sitting at the foot of the well in the midday sun, refusing to drink.

2

Eve as Everywoman:
Climate Grief as Global Solidarity

GRACE THOMAS

It's Holy Saturday, the day before Easter. A day weighted by grief and darkness. As a Church of England priest, I've been thinking about my sermon for tomorrow and I am struck by the painful irony of one of the themes that often accompanies the Easter talk – the centrality of women in the story. Normally, I would feel compelled to mention how all four Gospels agree that women were the first to see the empty tomb. Normally, I would celebrate this demonstration of disregard for the patriarchal, hierarchical conventions of first-century Jerusalem. Normally, but not today. Maybe because I am writing this sermon on a day thronged with loss and associated with darkness, I cannot see past the crushing reality that, despite the fact that Jesus continually defied the expectations of his peers, in our world today women still bear the brunt of burden and oppression. As climate breakdown threatens this fragile world, women will again be the ones who carry the greatest load and are heard the least. Our world is changing, but, it seems, some things stay the same.

A few years ago, I spent a short time with my cousin in Chennai, India, working with a charity that supported homeless women. These women were among the most disenfranchised and least visible in the city. A year later, Chennai was hit by terrible floods and as I saw Facebook images of my cousins wading through waist-high water, I wondered how the homeless women I had encountered were coping. The following year, Chennai was hit with a crippling drought, the ramifications of which are still ongoing. The implications for the poorest and the least visible are catastrophic.

It is an indisputable reality that women – and women in the majority world in particular – disproportionately experience the impact of the havoc caused by climate breakdown. Climate breakdown is recognized as creating higher levels of violence and abuse against women. Physical and sexual violence is used as a way of silencing female environmental campaigners, and children are married off in areas that have been affected by climate breakdown in order to help address family hardship.[1] Women and girls are often the last to eat or be rescued; they face greater health and safety risks as water and sanitation systems become compromised. It is women and girls who take on increased domestic and care work as resources dwindle.[2] On the thorny issue of population growth, research demonstrates that women and children in sub-Saharan Africa have scarce access to reproductive and maternal health opportunities now,[3] and this will only get worse in an age of climate crisis, where money and resources diminish further. This will undoubtedly mean more pregnancies, more risks and higher rates of maternal morbidity and mortality.

The weight of grief I feel for my sisters is heavy. Tomorrow, numerous sermons will extol the fact that women were the first witnesses. Much will be made of how this reminds us that women are not to be sidelined, not to be oppressed, not to be dismissed through patriarchy. But we are woefully ignorant of the lives of millions who bear the burden of 'progress' now and will continue to do in the future. We seem to ignore the voices and the

---

1 Fiona Harvey, 2020, 'Climate Breakdown "Is Increasing Violence against Women"', *The Guardian*, 29 January, www.theguardian.com/environment/2020/jan/29/climate-breakdown-is-increasing-violence-against-women, accessed 21/04/20.

2 'In Focus: Climate Action by, and for, Women', *UN Women*, www.unwomen.org/en/news/in-focus/climate-change, accessed 21/04/20.

3 Clara Pons-Duran, Anna Lucas, Ambar Narayan, Andrew Dabalen and Clara Menéndez, 2019, 'Inequalities in sub-Saharan African Women's and Girls' Health Opportunities and Outcomes: Evidence from the Demographic and Health Surveys', *Journal of Global Health*, 9(1), 010410, www.ncbi.nlm.nih.gov/pmc/articles/PMC6326483/, accessed 21/04/20.

plight of women and girls. I hear earnest climate campaigners in the UK talking about how they are acting for the sake of their grandchildren, and I want to cry out in despair for the forgotten lives of those people in our world right now, who, unseen and unacknowledged, are sinking deep into the muddy plains of our greed and wilful obliviousness. The balance of justice does not fall in favour of women. It repeatedly tips away, in a patriarchal reality that has woven itself through the story of time, right back to the woman in the garden. The woman named Eve.[4]

Eve. What is the story behind the person who holds the biblical title of being the first woman on earth? In the third chapter of Genesis, we hear how a crafty serpent spun a seductive tale to Eve about the benefits of eating fruit from the forbidden tree, and Eve took some of this fruit, gave it to her husband, who was with her, and they both ate it. When God found out, he responded by cursing the culprits. The first part of Eve's curse is generally understood to mean that she will have increased pain in childbearing, but it could be translated to mean, 'I will greatly increase your toil (that is, your physical work) and in grief you shall bring forth children (relating to the harsh reality of high childhood mortality in Ancient Near Eastern times)'. The second half of the curse relates to how Eve will be subordinate to male rule. Adam's curse relates wholly to the hardship of working the ground, the reality of which must not be underestimated, but this job is not something that only men do. Women throughout the ages have battled with and worked the ground. It seems that the curse relayed to Adam is far less than the curse meted out to Eve.

I have always been intrigued by this. So I began a journey of exploration into the meaning of the first woman mentioned in the Bible. My first encounter was with 'transgressor Eve' – the one so familiar to many of us. The writer of 1 Timothy identified Eve as the transgressor and suggested that, therefore, women should not exert authority over men (1 Timothy 2.12–14). Both Calvin and Wesley argued that even though Scripture suggests that Adam

---

4 Eve is not named until the end of Genesis 3 and Adam is not used as a pronoun at all in the first three chapters of Genesis. However, these names have become synonymous with the first humans and therefore, for the sake of clarity, will be used in this chapter.

was with Eve at the time of the taking of the forbidden fruit, this could not have been the case. Such a suggestion is simply not 'credible', Calvin asserted,[5] and Wesley claimed that the woman deviously manipulated him into eating the fruit and, had Adam been there earlier, he 'would have interposed to prevent the sin'.[6] Despite the lack of scriptural evidence for these assertions, the message is clear. As the feminist theologian Phyllis Trible acknowledges, traditional, misogynistic readings of Genesis have almost 'acquired a status of canonicity'.[7]

In a way, 'transgressor Eve' became a 'blueprint for Woman'.[8] She became 'everywoman' in the sense that the perception of Eve as untrustworthy, and therefore to be 'contained' by man, defined how all women were then perceived.[9] This perception has validated patriarchal notions of male leadership and female disempowerment. Despite influential people throughout history rallying against such notions – none more notable for Christians than Jesus – this perception of male dominance and female subjugation pervades many areas of our modern world. And it contributes to the situation we now find ourselves in, where women and girls are once again overlooked, disempowered and disproportionately affected by climate breakdown.

I want to propose a different way of viewing 'everywoman' Eve. One that could stand in solidarity with those women and girls in the midst of the climate gender imbalance. I began to see a woman who could speak into the grief born of frustration and injustice that continues to dominate this world. This new 'every-woman' Eve arose from a different way of approaching the texts in Genesis.

---

5 J. Calvin, 1578, *Commentaries on the Book of Genesis*, Vol. 1, Edinburgh: The Edinburgh Printing Company, p. 152.

6 J. Wesley, 1765, *Wesley's Notes on the Bible*, Christian Classics Ethereal Library, www.ccel.org/w/wesley/notes/, accessed 17/04/2020, p. 817.

7 Phyllis Trible, 1978, *God and the Rhetoric of Sexuality*, Philadelphia, PA: Fortress Press, p. 73.

8 Pamela Norris, 1999, *The Story of Eve*, London: Macmillan, p. 4.

9 Julie Faith Parker, 2013, 'Blaming Eve Alone: Translation, Omission, and Implications of צמה in Genesis 3:6b', *Journal of Biblical Literature* 4, pp. 729–47.

The creation narratives in Genesis are considered by many biblical scholars to be myths. Myths were used as a form of telling stories in Ancient Near Eastern (ANE) times. They communicated truth, even if they were not historically true. Myths gave meaning to life and explained the role for, and of, humans in the world.[10] The creation poem in Genesis 2—3 sought to explain the conditions of the author's context.[11] Carol Meyers has argued that Eve's primary purpose was to represent the woman of this era, an 'everywoman' for that time.[12] And this was a very different 'everywoman' to the one she became later.

Life for people in ancient Israel was hard. Tending the ground that produced little food was physically exhausting.[13] Women were expected to play their part in this hard labour, pregnant or not, and a combination of hard physical work, unforgiving living conditions, poor nutrition and limited access to health care resulted in high rates of prenatal and infant mortality.[14] The curse of Eve maps on to Meyers' concept of Eve as 'everywoman': women will toil, have multiple pregnancies and will endure anguish as a result. Women will struggle in their relationship with men. The curse of Eve parallels the struggles of ancient Israelite women, and her story gave the women a reason for why things were so hard. Eve was their 'everywoman'.

The contemporary impact of climate change upon women evokes the lives of ancient Israelite women. I can't help but see a solidarity between the world's most politically and economically marginalized women and the first woman. In journeying with Eve, I have found that she represents all women whose lives are immeasurably hard and who have little agency or voice. The struggles of Eve speak into the struggles of women in a time of climate crisis: their huge workload, lack of basic health care, lengthy and dangerous journeys for water and sanitation needs,

---

10 John W. Rogerson, R. W. L. Moberly and W. Johnstone, 2001, *Genesis and Exodus*, Sheffield: Sheffield Academic Press, p. 63.

11 Rogerson et al., *Genesis and Exodus*, p. 114.

12 C. Meyers, 2012, *Rediscovering Eve: Ancient Israelite Women in Context*, Oxford: Oxford University Press, p. 3.

13 P. Davies and J. Rogerson, 2005, *The Old Testament World*, 2nd edn, Louisville, KY: Westminster John Knox Press, pp. 17–19.

14 Meyers, *Rediscovering Eve*, p. 96.

and their lack of power within a patriarchal context. Eve's life and experience just as easily speaks into the lives of many women today as she did to women over two and a half thousand years ago. The idea that myths help to explain the world around us is not a way to validate the situation – to make it acceptable – but, instead, a way to give understanding and, therefore, a sense of belonging to a wider community. A sense of 'togetherness' and a comfort in knowing you are not alone. A recognition that the story of many women and girls today is not a new story but an ancient one. Expressing grief for a dying world and grief for the plight of our sisters is the first step to offering a response of solidarity. Eve as everywoman steps through time, looks at her sisters today and nods in understanding.

To the women straining every muscle, digging, planting, pruning and picking in a battle with the broken earth: Everywoman Eve stands with you.

To the woman climate campaigners, brutally silenced and forced to comply: Everywoman Eve gently sits with you and sighs in recognition.

To the young girls, married off to reduce the burden on their family: Everywoman Eve's tears fall with yours.

To the women whose bodies are wracked by injury following multiple births, whose hearts ache for the children lost, and whose hands struggle to feed the children they have: Everywoman Eve wraps her arms around you and shares your pain.

To the women last to be fed, last to be taught, last to be saved, last to be heard: Everywoman Eve hears you. She knows.

3

Ko Au te Whenua, Ko te Whenua Ko Au: I am the Land and the Land is Me

CHRISTOPHER DOUGLAS-HURIWAI

Relationship is the chief concern in the Māori mind. Our world view, perspective, ways of being and everyday life have their foundation, and indeed are deeply rooted in the idea of relationship. This relationship is not only restricted to other tribes, other Māori, or even other New Zealanders, but rather to everyone and everything. These connections and relationships are intimately related through the bonds of *whanaungatanga*. *Whanaungatanga*, writes Hirini Moko Mead, 'embraces whakapapa (genealogy) and focuses on relationships'. He goes on to say that 'the whanaungatanga principle reached beyond actual whakapapa'.[1] This reach of *whanaungatanga* beyond ourselves, beyond our nuclear family and out into the world, brings the whole world into relationship with one another, even more than that, in the Māori world view, it brings all of creation into relationship with God.

For Māori, *whenua* is the starting point for this story of relationship. *Whenua* is the term usually translated to mean land, but really speaks to the sum total of creation. It is a word with several meanings. However, all of those meanings speak to the importance of connectedness and relationship. Perhaps the most fundamental meaning, and certainly the most formational meaning associated with the word *whenua*, is 'placenta'. Mead writes: 'The whenua is the medium, between mother and child, that succours new life. After birth, whenua, as land succours the

---

1 Hirini Mead, 2003, *Tikanga Maori: Living by Maori Values*, Wellington: Huia, p. 28.

whanau (family).'[2] It is customary, following the birth of a child, for the placenta to be taken to the ancestral lands of the family to be buried. *Whenua* as placenta and *whenua* as land therefore work together to create an everlasting identity. Through this practice, an unbreakable bond is established between the child and the land, establishing the child's place in the world and providing the fertile ground from which the child's *pepeha* is enabled to emerge.

> *Ko Hikurangi te Maunga*
> *Ko Waiapu te Awa*
> *Ko Ngati Porou te Iwi*

Pepeha are tribal sayings that articulate the identity story of a people through the lens of the natural world. For example, the pepeha written above, my pepeha, identifies me as a person from the Ngati Porou tribal region. Literally, this pepeha says, 'Hikurangi is the Mountain, Waiapu is the River, Ngati Porou is the Tribe'. This example clearly shows the interplay between *whenua*, that is to say creation, and identity. For Ngati Porou and other tribes across Aotearoa (New Zealand), pepeha are not just statements of place, they are statements of identity. An identity that is deeply rooted in the land and space of our ancestors. It is an identity that draws on the dominant geographical features of our region as a way of articulating belonging and connection. Paraone Gloyne notes the importance of pepeha when he says, 'Pepeha is your identity as expressed through your maunga, awa, moana, tūpuna, and iwi. Pepeha is your own intrinsic brand of who you are, created in the realms of the divine, before birth, personified in your being, and lasting for evermore.'[3]

It must be said, however, that pepeha are not just drawing on mountains and rivers as simple geographic markers, but rather, within the tradition of pepeha, these natural features are ancestors from whom Māori trace our descent. It is in this way that Māori

---

2 Mead, *Tikanga Maori*, p. 288.

3 Paraone Gloyne, 2020, 'Pepeha', *Buy Maori Made* (post), 13 May, www.facebook.com/groups/buymaorimade/permalink/243454007003080/, accessed 17/08/20.

are once again brought into relationship with the natural world. This reality is reflected in the stories and histories of our people, so we name these natural features; they are given personalities and stories, they are treated as a living, breathing part of our genealogy. Indeed, in some instances these mountains and rivers are afforded legal personhood, as was the case in 2017 with the Whanganui river in the North Island of New Zealand being granted the same legal rights, privileges and protections as a living person.[4]

So while it may seem as though pepeha are simple statements of identity and nothing more, a deeper understanding of the subject soon reveals that it is not just a matter of physical identity and descent that is at stake but a spiritual and divine identity too. This is perhaps most poignantly seen in Henare Tate's Foundational Concepts, which names three aspects of the Māori reality that define Māori identity: *Atua* (God), *Tangata* (Humanity) and *Whenua* (Creation). Of these three Foundational Concepts, Henare Tate notes, 'In Māori consciousness these three sets of relationships constitute who we are.'[5] That is to say that, without these three concepts, Māori as a people cannot exist. Of these three, however, Henare Tate privileges Atua as standing at the head of this Māori trinity of identity, and it is through relationship with Atua that land is raised to prominence in the Māori world view. Henare Tate explains by saying, 'When we refer to whenua we include all realities in their own complex relationship with Atua.'[6] Henare Tate names these relationship links whanaungatanga, further strengthening the point that Atua, that is to say God, is the source of all relationship and the reason whenua is so important to Māori identity, saying, 'For Māori the genealogy of the human race and therefore the lines of whanaungatanga begin with Io-Matua-Kore (a traditional name for God), the parentless one. Io-Matua-Kore is the source of all

---

4 Isaac Davison, 2017, 'Whanganui River Given Legal Status of a Person under Unique Treaty of Waitangi Settlement', *NZ Herald*, 15 March, www.nzherald.co.nz/nz/news/article.cfm?c_id=1&objectid=11818858, accessed 01/06/20.

5 Henare Tate, 2012, *He Puna Iti i Te Ao Marama: A Little Spring in the World of Light*, Auckland: Libro International, p. 38.

6 Tate, *He Puna Iti i Te Ao Marama*, p. 40.

whanaungatanga.'[7] With these realities in mind it soon becomes clear that climate change, along with its negative impact on creation, is not only an issue of personal identity and sovereignty, but also spiritual identity and sovereignty. It should come as no surprise that, for Māori, the negative impacts on land, the sea and waterways, and the threats to the environment represented by climate change, are a major source of trauma and indeed a threat to our very existence.

One of the most significant parts of our tribal area is known as the Waiapu Catchment. This is the area that includes both the ancestral river and ancestral mountain of my tribe. Within this area alone exists both key identity markers of my people and the sum total of our pepeha. The Waiapu Catchment is of immense spiritual and cultural significance to my people; however, since the turn of the nineteenth century, it has been under threat. Initially this threat came in the form of the large-scale clearing, burning and felling of the native forest and bush that covered and sustained the Waiapu Catchment and its people. This clearing inevitably led to land erosion, sediment build-up and huge environmental change within the catchment. In more recent times, however, it is the various effects of climate change that attack the heart of the Waiapu Catchment and its people.

As the Waiapu Catchment continues to be negatively impacted by the effects of climate change, the people in turn are negatively impacted. The ancient saying of our people, *Ko au te awa, ko te awa ko au*, literally translated as 'I am the river and the river is me', speaks to this symbiotic relationship between Māori and the natural world. For Māori, creation is not just somewhere we live, or a commodity to be traded in, but is rather a reflection of ourselves. When creation hurts, we hurt. When creation thrives, we thrive. Pepeha, and the reality it speaks to, is not a metaphor but a statement of truth. When we say *Ko Hikurangi te Maunga, Ko Waiapu te Awa*, we are really saying 'I AM Hikurangi', 'I AM Waiapu'. It is for this reason that for my people, and indeed Māori across Aotearoa, climate change proposes not only a

---

7 Henare Tate, 2002, 'Stepping into Maori Spirituality', in *Spirituality in Aotearoa New Zealand: Catholic Voices*, Auckland: Accent, p. 42.

threat to our economic capital but also a threat to our cultural and spiritual capital and well-being as a people.

Climate change and its associated impacts bring with it not just environmental changes but an anxiety that, as our natural landscape is damaged, so too is the pepeha of our people. The idea that these damages to our pepeha may be irreversible is almost too much to bear for the descendants of the Waiapu Catchment because it is not only our settlements, homes and communities at stake but our very existence as people of the Waiapu Valley. Settlements can be re-established, homes rebuilt and communities re-formed. The cultural, spiritual and tribal identity of an entire people, however, is not as easily repaired. As the Psalmist notes,[8] it is unthinkable, even impossible, to sing the songs of your people, the songs of God, in a foreign land. How much more unimaginable must it be therefore to comprehend your existence as a people of the land and indeed as a people of God when the very creation that not only tells you who you are, but tells you how you are connected in relationship to God, is under threat. Living in the foreboding shadow of these threats turned reality not only has an impact on the day-to-day lives of my people, but our emotional and mental well-being as well. The anxiety of the unknown, the grief of loss, the unfathomable realization that the intergenerational transmission of identity, of knowledge, of spiritual inter-connectedness that has sustained our people for generations may be brought to an abrupt end, all rests heavy on the shoulders of my people.

The spiritual reality of my people was for ever changed in late 1833 when Piripi Taumataakura, himself a descendant of Ngati Porou, returned to the Waiapu Valley following a period of captivity in the northern districts of the North Island. During this period, Taumataakura came under the influence of the Church Missionary Society and their missionaries who had been active in the north since 1814.[9] Taumataakura's freedom was ultimately secured through the influence of these missionaries, and he

---

8 Psalm 137.4.

9 Alan Davidson, 2004, *Christianity in Aotearoa New Zealand: A History of Church and Society in New Zealand*, 3rd edn, Wellington: Education for Ministry, p. 8.

returned to the Waiapu Valley not only with a new perspective but a new God. Although initial success was sparse, Taumataakura planted the seed of the gospel deep in the fertile land of his people. This enabled, and indeed empowered, the growth of a truly indigenous expression of Christianity, one that not only endures to this day but saw Māori cosmologies, understandings and perspectives placed alongside their biblical counterparts. This resulted in the birthing of a church that likewise respected and valued the cultural capital of my people. The return home of Taumataakura with the gospel in hand meant our first exposure to the faith came, in a way, from ourselves. Despite this, there remained tensions between the Church and the people of the Waiapu Valley, largely stemming from the role, both perceived and real, that missionaries played in the colonization of Aotearoa New Zealand. Navigating these relationships now is made easier because historic relationship exists; indeed these relationships have embedded themselves in the very *whakapapa* of my people. Once again we see the power of *whanaungatanga*, those unbreakable lines of relationship, bringing itself to bear in such a way that the interests and integrity of the people, the land and God are not only privileged but protected.

Our identity as a people deeply connected to the land is reflected in the name we traditionally used for ourselves. Although we as indigenous people of Aotearoa New Zealand are now generally known as 'Māori', a word meaning 'normal' or 'natural', in pre-contact times we understood ourselves as *Tangata Whenua* (People of the Land). Huriwai and Tamihere note:

> As tangata whenua, people of the land, the natural environment is of foundational importance to Māori identity. Seeing themselves as being in a *whakapapa* relationship with the whole created order, a Māori worldview has recognised over generations that their relationship with and kaitiekitanga (guardianship) responsibility to the physical and spiritual wellbeing of the natural environment is inextricably bound to their own physical and spiritual wellbeing.[10]

---

10 Michael Tamihere and Christopher Douglas-Huriwai, 2019, 'Atua, Tangata, Whenua: God, Maori, and Creation', The Anglican Church in Aotearoa, New Zealand and Polynesia, p. 9.

Thus, although the argument may be put that my people have yet to feel the full impact of climate change upon both our natural environment and indeed our cultural and spiritual well-beings, the impending threat is, in and of itself, sufficient to constitute a legitimate source of both climate grief and anxiety.

From land loss to racism, to cultural annihilation and systemic injustice, my people have felt the full force of assimilation and colonization working together in an attempt to alienate us from our cultural history, our spiritual connectedness and our place in creation. Through the resilience of our elders and the commitment of our storytellers, our knowledge keepers and our tribal protectors, my people have managed to weather the storms of injustice from the very beginnings of European settlement in Aotearoa. The latest threat to our cultural and spiritual tradition, however, may be too big a challenge for my people to overcome. The ancient saying of our people, '*Whatu ngarongaro he tangata, toitu he whenua* – People perish, but the land remains',[11] speaks to the Māori understanding of the permanence not only of land but of the intergenerational transmission of everything the land, and indeed all of creation, connects us to: our history, our ancestors and our God. Living now on the edge of a new reality, a reality that casts a shadow of doubt over this ancient saying and understanding of our people, has us not only questioning our ancestral knowledge and wisdom but indeed our very future as a people. The anxiety we experience now in the face of climate change is unlike any other threat we have experienced in the past. It is this threat of irreparable cultural and spiritual loss that is the source not only of the climate grief we now experience but the cultural and spiritual grief too. As seemingly overwhelming as those historic, colonial threats were, the onus was on my people, and my people alone, to determine the outcome of those challenges. Climate change, however, brings with it a new dynamic, a dynamic that requires not just my people doing all we can to push back against climate change, but that everybody, everywhere commit similarly. The future of my people depends on it.

---

11 Sidney M. Mead and Neil Grove, 2001, *Nga pepeha a nga tipuna: The Sayings of the Ancestors*, Wellington, NZ: Victoria University Press, p. 425.

4

Johane Masowe:
An African Man of Sorrows

ISABEL MUKONYORA

When it comes to Africa, the ecological crisis is a human-caused problem hard to solve because of the profound way that European settlers destroyed indigenous religions and cultures across the continent. While some of the white settlers used guns to expropriate fertile farmland from Africans, others requisitioned cheap labour for handling their industrial tools for the mass production of crops, cattle ranching, mining and building towns, roads, railway lines, urban homes and so on. Johane Masowe (1914–73) was born into a context where Africans had lost control of their religion and ecology, culture and sense of belonging, becoming dispossessed members of a world built extracting wealth to profit Western civilization. The ruthless pursuit of wealth from extractive industries in particular destroyed so much of the African sense of belonging that Africans began to question European missionary talk about the God of dominion. The transnational Johane Masowe (John of the Wilderness) Apostles Church began with an African man whose personal experiences of pain and suffering caused him to revisit the original stories of suffering, humility, healing and the hope for eco-justice that comes out of gospel stories of Jesus and his first followers.

Johane Masowe started preaching the gospel as he understood it by listening to stories about John the Baptist and Jesus with *vanhu vatema*, 'black people', in mind. He embodied grief with images of margins of the cityscapes of Israel giving him the liminal spaces to speak openly about God for the disenfranchised poor and sick. Johane Masowe deeply questioned Western orthodoxy by turning the spiritual problems of displacement in creation into an opportunity to dramatize knowledge about the biblical God protecting the lives of black children wandering in the wilderness throughout colonial Africa.[1]

Johane Masowe is thus the Shona name of the founder of a Church who associated the Bible with social histories of victims of oppression. Today, there are thousands of followers in urban Zimbabwe, South Africa, Botswana, Zambia, Malawi, Tanzania, Kenya, and parts of the United Kingdom.[2] His followers meet wherever there are margins of cityscapes, allowing them to walk and do their theology by sharing experiences of reality. They reflect critically on questions about morality in wider society, remove shoes and pray under the sacred sky to feel the presence of the Creator. This gives meaning to interdependence with the *masowe*: liminal places or thresholds for the self-disclosure of *Mwari*, an ecological deity who gives the believer a sense of belonging, peace and justice.

Born in 1914 or 1915 on a colonial reserve territory in the Makoni District near Rusape, Johane Masowe lived in Gandanzara, meaning 'the Land of Hunger', a name highlighting the existential problem of living under colonial rule. He started preaching during the early 1930s – a difficult time of worldwide economic depression, a drought and an outbreak of cholera in Rhodesia (Zimbabwe). Johane did not hide the role of European missionaries in his life. He was given the baptismal name 'Peter' by the Anglican Church and he grew up under the care of his uncle, a minister in the John Wesleyan Methodist Church. He received his first Bible from a Catholic priest in Salisbury (Harare), telling one of his followers:

I associate myself with the Roman Catholic Church, although I have no permission of any representative of this church to preach to natives on their behalf. It is my intention to gather

---

1 Isabel Mukonyora, 2007, *Wandering the Gendered Wilderness: Suffering and Healing in an African Church*, New York: Peter Lang. See book cover.

2 Isabel Mukonyora, 2006, 'African Diaspora Within', in R. Marie Griffith and Barbara Dianne Savage (eds), *Women and Religion in the Diaspora*, Baltimore, MD: Johns Hopkins University Press, pp. 59–80.

natives around me and then obtain the necessary authority of the Roman Catholic Church to have a separate native Church.[3]

Like other youths of his time, Johane went to school at a mission station in Gandanzara. In addition to suffering from an illness that caused him a lot of pain, he witnessed *kufa nenzara*, meaning people 'dying' of hunger or famished on account of the unfair distribution of fertile land to Europeans, including missionaries who needed land to build schools, churches and hospitals. As Zimbabwe faced the ecological crisis of the 1930s, European missionaries started seeing their first generation of converts become young adults with questions about the purpose of worshipping God in a world full of oppression and the destruction of planetary life.[4] Johane made the connection between personal experiences of *kufa nekurwara* (dying of sickness) and ecological destruction.[5]

Johane's ministry began with 'hearing the voice' of God as Mwari in Shona language. He described himself as *kufa nekurwara*, or 'dying of pain', a common experience of people prone to get sick without money to pay for Western medicine. Johane was ill on many occasions in his life. In Shona, the word *kufa* describes death and eco-suffering in general. The same word also describes discomfort caused by sickness, hunger, thirst, heat, cold or even fear and ignorance. This was a lived theology for healing the earth against the background of much suffering. John of the Wilderness became the embodiment of knowledge about grief, from which he healed physically, emotionally, mentally and spiritually.

Before the decision to travel far and wide, Johane's spiritual journey took him around the margins of industrial parks, the Hunyani River and other urban areas frequented by Africans standing in queues for employment in Zimbabwe. One day, the

---

3 Clive M. Dillon-Malone SJ, 1978, *The Korsten Basketmakers: A Study of the Masowe Apostles, An Indigenous African Religious Movement*, Manchester: Manchester University Press, pp. 14–15.

4 Mukonyora, 'African Diaspora Within', pp. 59–80.

5 Isabel Mukonyora, 2008, 'Masowe Migration: A Quest for Liberation in the African Diaspora', *Religion Compass* 2, 10.1111.

police found him preaching with neither a pass from a white employer nor proof that he was representing one of the European-led churches. Johane later recounted to the police:

> I heard voices telling me that I was John. I had never been called by that name before. I thought that I was meant to be called John the Baptist. I therefore use that name. I think that name was given to me so that I should preach to the natives. I think that I was given the name, John the Baptist by Mwari.[6]

The diaspora within[7]

Partly out of fear of persecution for his radical acceptance of Mwari as an ecological deity, the African man of sorrows continued to wander around the margins of other cityscapes with rivers, lakes and dams used for *Jorodani* (Jordan River baptisms). By adopting the name of a biblical figure who used the margins of cityscapes for prayer, Johane dramatized his Christian response to the global spread of our ecological crisis by transforming the margins of cityscapes into liminal spaces for Africans to share their experiences in their mother tongue. To this day, the followers of John of the Wilderness wander on unoccupied pieces of land wedged between industrial parks and African townships without worrying about European missionary-established churches. These are places known to be continually plagued by toxic fumes and contaminants entering the soil and water. For example, Marimba Hill is a short distance from African townships in Harare, and right next to the industrial park attracting African workers for all sorts of manufacturing companies with huge storage facilities for coal and rubbish dumps of toxic industrial waste. Johane Masowe dramatized his own suffering and

---

6 Mukonyora, 'Masowe Migration'. Mwari means 'The One Who Is', that is, the mystery that explains prayers for healing and understanding God in nature.

7 Mukonyora, 'Masowe Migration', p. 59. By this term I meant to draw attention to both the loss of identity caused by colonial conquest and the rise of urban faith communities whose members welcomed worshipping God on the margins of cityscapes on the continent of Africa.

death to draw attention to the healing power of the biblical God of the people of Israel, who appeared to him as the Shona ecological deity Mwari.

Among the people who became majority members of the wilderness church were women of the urban wilderness. Throughout the social history of Zimbabwe, some women have run away from reserves where the only jobs available were the unpaid ones of farming, fetching firewood, cooking traditional food and brewing beer. The urban wilderness was conveniently placed for runaway women to use their traditional cooking skills to establish informal trading relations with otherwise alienated male workers going to and from the industrial areas.

Between 1943 and 1947, Johane Masowe travelled from Gandanzara to Bulawayo, then crossed the border into Botswana until he reached the Transvaal. After wandering from place to place, Johane and a group of his immediate followers, including a large number of women, decided to settle in a remote squatter area called Korsten, near Port Elizabeth, South Africa.[8] Bengt Sundkler describes this establishment of the Masowe community as inspired by 'a spirit of enterprise and collective energy borne out of protest against the white caste'.[9] Masowe Apostles discreetly lived for nearly 15 years on a salty swamp facing the Indian Ocean; illegal immigrants in South Africa.[10] Sustained by ideas of the self-disclosure of God, Johane became the leader of diasporic Africans on the margins of cityscapes. During the early 1960s the government of South Africa discovered that Masowe Apostles were illegal immigrants with ideas, and worked with colonial authorities in Zimbabwe to repatriate them to a Seke township on the outskirts of Harare. This did not stop John of the Wilderness from living in exile. He decided to lead some of his followers north, across the border between Zimbabwe and Zambia, where he settled in the copper-mining town called Ndola. Leaving behind followers starting to differ in their opinions about life in the wilderness, Johane Masowe died on 13 September 1973.

---

8 Dillon-Malone, *The Korsten Basketmakers.*

9 Bengt Sundkler, 1961, *Bantu Prophets of South Africa*, 2nd edn, Oxford: Oxford University Press, p. 324.

10 Dillon-Malone, *The Korsten Basketmakers*, pp. 40–1.

I write this during another economic depression, the corona-virus pandemic, and in the aftermath of the deadliest tropical cyclone on record, catastrophically damaging ecosystems and causing a humanitarian crisis in Mozambique, eastern Zimbabwe and Malawi in 2019. According to the World Health Organiza-tion, tropical cyclone Idai left 1,300 people dead and many more missing. This is in addition to human acts of oppression, vio-lence, economic poverty and the spread of diseases and social upheavals in many parts of post-colonial Africa. I welcome this opportunity to tell this African story of a contemporary response to the gospel as a message of hope for people now faced with climate change.

By transforming open-air margins of urban areas where the destruction of ecosystems took place into sacred sites for communing with God, Johane Masowe and his many followers are teaching contemporary Christians to become more deeply sensitized to the global signs of climate and ecological grief. Since my encounter with Masowe Apostles, my way of thinking has shifted from beginning with the God of Dominion associated with colonial missions to that of an ecological Source of Life easily misunderstood by human beings in the history of Christianity. My lifestyle and intellectual pursuits are now more focused on decolonizing our relationships with the earth than they have ever been. Church leaders could learn from the earth-centred liberation theology described above: the future of the Church does not depend on making money from destroying planetary life. Masowe Apostles have been able to revisit the meaning of God as the source of life on earth, evil as the destruction thereof and holistic healing as a description of salvation.

5

My Grandma's Oil Well

KYLE B. T. LAMBELET[1]

> We know that the whole creation has been groaning in labour pains until now. (Romans 8.22, NRSV)

I always found it strange that we had colour film of Grandma as a child. They weren't high quality, but from time to time during family gatherings my Uncle Kenny would pop in the VHS and we would watch blurry footage of her running with her sister Sue around the Garren family farm. My grandma's family was not wealthy, at least as I have come to understand. They owned and operated a small farm, and her dad Ray drove a delivery truck and sold Cub Cadet tractors. But the capacity to capture, develop and preserve moving pictures seemed an extravagant luxury for the late 1940s. It didn't fit with my understanding of her story.

My grandma went away for college, moving from Centralia, Illinois, to Enid, Oklahoma, to attend a Disciples of Christ school. It was there that she met my grandpa. They married and quickly started a family. When my dad, their first child, was born my grandma dropped out of college. After my dad, two more boys came quickly; and then, a few years later, Uncle Kenny.

When Kenny went to kindergarten, my grandmother went back to finish her degree at McPherson College. After a few years of night school, Grandma finished her degree and then went to work as an elementary teacher in Salina, Kansas, where my grandparents still live.

---

1 I wish to thank Francis Bonenfant, Karie Cross, Heather DuBois, Andrew Krinks, Nicole Lambelet, Nick Peterson and Allyn Steele, who all offered valuable feedback on this essay.

Grandma always taught in a school that served working-class folks, Whittier Elementary. She loved teaching children to read, so settled mostly in the first grade. Now in her retirement, Grandma remains busy by volunteering and keeping up with her family. She is one of the kindest people I have ever had the pleasure of knowing.

One day, I was riffling through Grandma's fridge, looking for something to eat (Grandma always stocked small luxuries we didn't have at home). Grandma was working through the mail.

'This is my monthly oil check,' Grandma told me.

'Oil check?' I asked.

'It's been split between so many descendants now that it doesn't amount to much. But, I get about $400 a month from the oil well on the old Murray land.'

It was an off-handed comment, like talking about the weather. It was not a disclosure of concern or confession of guilt. It was just commentary on the normal, everyday happenings of her life.

I didn't fully understand the significance of her admission in that moment of revelation. I'm still not sure that I do. But gaps in the story now made sense: the colour film, the move to Oklahoma, surviving the lean years, returning to school, small cash gifts to the family. All these details became clearer with the backdrop of a little extra money from her family oil well.

Grandma's grandparents, the Murrays, discovered oil on their land in Centralia in 1939.[2] My grandmother was four at the time. As the film testifies, the oil well provided an economic boon for the Murray and Garren families. Many of the details of that story are lost from our family lore. But the film remains an artefact, a physical product and material representation of the largesse of fossil capitalism.[3] As a result, oil becomes a connecting theme in my grandma's story. The oil, drawn from a well on land once occupied by the Tamoroa tribe of the Illiniwek, came steadily and provided a modest supplement to this middle-class,

---

2 For a history of the entanglement of oil and Christianity in the United States, see Darren Dochuk, 2019, *Anointed with Oil: How Christianity and Crude Made Modern America*, New York: Basic Books.

3 Andreas Malm, 2016, *Fossil Capital: The Rise of Steam-Power and the Roots of Global Warming*, London: Verso.

white family. Oil and the revenue from its exploitation illumin-
ates key moments in my grandma's narrative, and in my story
as well.

What am I to do with this thread in my family story? The
question becomes especially acute as I have come to see with ever
greater clarity the real costs of fossil fuel exploitation: rising global
temperatures, melting sea ice, biodiversity loss, mass extinction,
climate instability, human displacement, extreme weather – the
list could go on. These global environmental effects, moreover,
are the manifestations of a domestic racialized economy in
which white settlers occupied native lands, at the behest of the
federal government, and benefited from its exploitation. Climate
degradation and settler-colonial capitalism are bound up with
one another, two sides of the same coin. But such attributions,
truthful though they may be, can leave these problems distant
and abstract. My grandma's oil well grafts the reality of climate
catastrophe into my own story. It is not something distant, but
something near, bound to my very blood and bones.

One response could be repression. I could simply erase that
detail and appreciate the gifts of my grandma's story. I can
reconstruct a hagiography of her life that cordons off the fact of
her oil well as insignificant. We all do this in our self-narrations.
We never include all the details. Our stories always involve
omissions, those known and unknown, and I could strategically
omit some details in this self-narration.[4] But repressed details
often come out otherwise. In repressing my own complicity in
our current climate catastrophe, I may participate in placing all
responsibility on another guilty party – such as oil executives –
and in so doing avoid reckoning with my own culpability. But
the colour film remains, evidence that repression cannot subdue.

Another option may be denunciation. I could critique my
grandma for her complicity. I could question her willingness
to continue benefiting from the exploitation of fossil fuels and
denounce her collection of her monthly cheque. I might issue a
Jeremiad against her, showing how her actions are connected to

---

4 Such opacity can be the ground for taking responsibility. See Judith
Butler, 2005, *Giving an Account of Oneself*, 1st edn, New York: Fordham
University Press.

the exploitation of the earth and the displacement of people of colour, demanding that she take responsibility. Yet, such rejection participates perversely in the same aspiration as repression: seeking to purify my own story at the expense of another, in this case my grandmother.

Neither of these options, repression or denunciation, seems faithful. Neither of these options keeps faith with my grandma nor with the call of the gospel. Both repression and denunciation attempt to maintain a kind of purity, distancing my story from the contamination of oil. In an ironic way they join with the dynamic of racialized purity to obfuscate the complex dynamics – racial, economic and environmental – that created the problem in the first place.

I cannot unsee the film and unknow the truth about Grandma's well. It pollutes each part of her story, clinging like oil to a common seabird who has dived into a slick. If neither repression nor denunciation keeps faith, what option remains?

Lament.

Lament is one of Scripture's primary modes of prayer. The psalms are full of them; it's the most common genre of Scripture's prayer book.[5] God laments over creation before the flood; Rachel weeps over her children; Jeremiah cries out in exile; Job denounces God's abusive sovereignty. Jesus draws from the laments of the psalms to issue his last words, 'My God, my God, why have you forsaken me?' Laments are prayers at the end of human agency.[6] They confront the reality of our situation in recognition that things are not as they should be.

Even as prayers of lament have form, they are at times chaotic. The book of Lamentations, for example, takes poetic form only to have the narrator break it down.[7] Laments are messy prayers, polluted prayers. They acknowledge many actors – enemies,

---

5 Glenn Pemberton, 2012, *Hurting with God: Learning to Lament with the Psalms*, Abilene, TX: Abilene Christian University Press.

6 Kyle B. T. Lambelet, 2019, 'How Long O Lord: Practices of Lamentation and the Restoration of Political Agency', in Joshua Burns, Michael Cover and John Thiede (eds), *Bridging Scripture and Moral Theology: Essays in Dialogue with Yiu Sing Lúcás Chan, S.J.*, Lanham, MD: Rowman & Littlefield.

7 Kathleen M. O'Connor, 2002, *Lamentations and the Tears of the World*, Maryknoll, NY: Orbis Books.

God, self, neighbour – and identify how we are all tangled up in a situation that no one can put right.

Climate grief – mourning the actual and anticipated loss of ecological systems and our place in them – is a form of mourning that might learn something from this scriptural practice of lament. Climate grief, often repressed or denounced, comes out otherwise when we displace our desire for purity on to others. The cleansing tears of lamentation allow me to see the moving pictures I've inherited through a new lens. The polluted prayers of lamentation offer me a way to tarry with my inheritance, remaining in its ruins.

Learning to lament the planetary deaths we are living through, for me, has meant grappling with this truth: the modes of flourishing that I have inherited – good rhythms of vocation, community, care – are implicated inextricably in the racialized destruction of the earth. My grandmother's beautiful life, which exemplifies these goods, is also a life enabled inescapably by the exploitation of fossil fuels. But to bring this truth even closer, my own life is similarly polluted. There is no way to account for the gifts I have received of education, financial security and vocational fulfilment without a backdrop of environmental degradation, without my grandma's oil well.

So, I lament. I lament my loss of innocence, my inability to repress or denounce and thereby remove the stain from my story. I lament my own awkward and unearned complicity in fossil fuel exploitation. It would be easy to point to those one-percenters who have made obscene wealth from fossil fuel extraction, processing, sale and use. Clearly, these actors are enemies of the earth and those creature-kind who live here. But what is more difficult is to turn the spectre of judgement back on ourselves – on myself. I operate with constrained agency: no one ever asked me if I would like to benefit from the oil still pumping from the ground on the old Murray farm in Centralia, Illinois. Yet, pump it does, and benefit I do.

Such lament induces yet another temptation: resignation. I might throw up my hands and say my inheritance is polluted and there is nothing I can do. Like repression and denunciation, this operates as yet another strategy of escape, where I refuse to allow lament to do its deepest work. While I can learn from the laments of Scripture, I am positioned differently. Too often the tendency of those of us with subject-position privilege place ourselves in the positions of the marginalized or the prophet. Rather than the poor crying out for justice, I would do better to read myself as David, confronted by Nathan for his sin. Rather than daughter Zion of the book of Lamentations, in my privilege I am better analogized as the narrator, first ignoring her cry from a distance but later drawn into solidarity and even self-accusation.[8] The scriptural response to resignation is repentance, turning towards the God who can redeem us and convert us towards reparation and solidarity with those ground up by our violence.[9]

Repentance acknowledges that, indeed, there is nothing I can do to purify myself and my story. So, I turn with faith to the God who is still creating, sustaining and redeeming. Praying that God will 'wash me thoroughly from my iniquity, and cleanse me from my sin' (Psalm 51.2, NRSV) moves me beyond a hope in personal purity. Rather, I put my faith in that which I cannot see, that God is working even to the seventh generation.

Reparation, then, includes free acts of grace that follow from repentance. Such repair ought not to regress into merely an economic exchange, yet another repetition of the capitalist logic of purity. I cannot purchase my redemption by adding up the total amount of birthday and Christmas gifts from my grandma and donating it to the climate justice movement in order to expiate my oil-stained sins, as so much good-white-folk-activity attempts. If only it were so simple! The work of lament invites us to stay with the trouble, not cutting short the real grief that we rightly feel, so that acts of repentance and reparation might flow as a grace-filled response rather than a begrudging exchange.[10] Here in the Anthropocene, in this era of human making, we reach the end of

---

8 O'Connor, *Lamentations and the Tears of the World*.

9 I have learned especially from Jennifer Harvey's critique of too-easy-hopes for reconciliation among white folk and the need for repentance and repair. See Jennifer Harvey, 2014, *Dear White Christians: For Those Still Longing for Racial Reconciliation*, Grand Rapids, MI: Eerdmans.

10 I borrow this phrase from Donna Jeanne Haraway, 2016, *Staying with the Trouble: Making Kin in the Chthulucene*, Durham, NC: Duke University Press.

KYLE B. T. LAMBELET

our capacities to unmake the strange world we have constructed. As such, acts of reparation participate in a hope that outstrips those very acts.

And so, I lament in hope. Lament draws me into petition, struggle, solidarity and hope, with a God who is still creating. Lament allows me to tarry with the stain, keeping faith with my grandma, with those human and other creatures our oil exploitation has harmed, and with generations yet unborn. Lament nurtures a hope for something that I cannot yet see, but I can actively wait and work for. As Paul stated, 'we know that the whole creation has been groaning in labour pains until now' (Romans 8.22, NRSV). I hear that groaning nowhere more acutely than in the steady, rhythmic creak of my grandmother's oil well.

6

This Stone will be a
Witness against Us

JON SEALS

I am interested in how we manifest the ineffable. This curiosity towards that which cannot be described has guided me to work with and be inspired by natural materials that contain embedded layers of meaning built through time. Natural materials speak in many ways: one way is through echo – our own voice bounces back at us, and, if we are receptive, we notice how the contours of the message take on a new shape during this mysterious transaction. I've witnessed our noise, our transgressions, be absorbed, forgiven, nearly entirely by natural materials. At other times our actions appear to reverberate outwards into a great abyss.

It is instinct to protect ourselves from exterior dangers, and so we imitate and practise through play when young. This begins a curious relationship to our natural environments; we realize we must respect our surroundings and we are also tempted to exploit them to serve our own needs and desires. I have a distinct mid-summer memory of digging into the ground next to my home and creating a little hole to sit in as a child. Children often make shelters or 'forts' when given time to play in nature. I can clearly recall the silence when submerged beneath the surface of the earth. As if sound itself came to the soil to die.

A child of Eastern Kentucky, I shot tin cans for target practice with rifles against a rolling nearby bluff, sprays of bullets taken into the earth round after round as if nothing had happened seconds before. Soil takes our noise; it takes our aggression, our violence. However, the sound of those same gunshots bounce off the surface of the ground and echo through canyons and hollows, heard and felt by everyone for miles. The earth has the capacity to shelter and absorb our blows, but also to trumpet, accentuate and reveal. It takes our secrets and makes them public if it so desires. Water, rocks, soil and air receive what they are given and bear witness, testifying to the weight of their burden.

The rocks do have agency, and they do cry out. Organic materials have previous lives, have witnessed and participated in countless stories. By their nature they have been born of destruction and death, which yield new life, and historically this sacred system has operated on its own terms. Today there is a new death, the death of cycle. The circle is cut and bent into line, and there is a new kind of beginning and there is a new kind of end.

My family's history maps the history of these endings. First, there was coal: bald mountains and hills – disfigured through mining. Loved ones under collapsed tunnels, lungs damaged beyond repair by fine dust, displaced wildlife, deforestation. Today a new saviour emerges: fracking for oil deposits. Just a few years ago, large machines systematically covered the countryside on US highways and routes near my childhood home. The machines parked and extended long steel arms for bracing themselves to strike the ground with such force homes throughout the region shook as if by an earthquake. Walls and foundations cracked. The earth would take on this blow but not forgive it. Instead, it issued an aggressive warning. Subterranean vibrations carried for miles. Digging holes for protection might also become holes that bury. The protection the earth extends also becomes the mechanism for its own defence.

The earth is not passive. It bears witness and provides testimony to God. Its wounds reveal the spirit and the sin of the ages. In the book of Joshua, the narrator describes a covenant between God and the tribes of Israel. Joshua selects and places a large stone to which agency is given to testify to God and to people:

On that day Joshua made a covenant for the people, and there at Shechem he reaffirmed for them decrees and laws. And Joshua recorded these things in the Book of the Law of God. Then he took a large stone and set it up there under the oak near the holy place of the LORD. 'See!' he said to all the people.

'This stone will be a witness against us. It has heard all the words the LORD has said to us. It will be a witness against you if you are untrue to your God.' (Joshua 24.25–27, NIV)

God calls a witness to the stand, a stone, to hold humans accountable to their covenant to one another and to God. Stones speak about our actions. We are being held accountable.

These grave realities are at times overwhelming and it can be difficult to know how to respond. Today I create mixed-media works with materials harvested directly from bodies of water and land with severe shifts in natural environments, including the Gulf of Mexico along Florida's Nature Coast, rural US Appalachia primarily in the state of Kentucky, and most recently along the Kankakee River, south of Chicago, Illinois, where, until a little over a century ago, there was an everglade as large as Florida's. Artworks are created by pouring, dipping and combining hand-drawn and painted elements using the materials collected. I work directly from the soil, water and plant life.

I've been able to identify surprising connections between seemingly disparate parts of the United States. These materials are collected from where I live and where my family is from. Through site-specific soil, sand and water, as well as particular materials, like tobacco and coal, I've been listening and trying to echo the wound and witness of the earth, to see how the environment and its elements give shape to my artistic voice. Featured in this publication are works using soil harvested from Kentucky. Throughout my training I've learned ways to use and bend and manipulate my materials, seeking to give order to them. However, I've noticed when my touch is light – when there is less of me, and more of the earth – the result is far more interesting. Early on, I could not get the material articulation I wanted with my own hands. In desperation I simply dipped paper into a large bucket of sludge – water from Florida's Gulf Coast, mixed with mud and coal dust from Kentucky. The edge of the dip, where clean paper met the soiled and wet paper, appeared like the ridge of a Kentucky mountain, but also like the roll of an ocean wave against the sky. My two homes became one. I let it drip dry, allowing gravity to do its work, and the soil materials catch against the grain of the paper. In several of the works, fractal patterns emerge after the materials dry, revealing a barren, dry land. A scene that recalls bald caps left by the process of mountaintop mining. Of course, this is my own echo, shaped by listening and letting the materials follow their course. But it is a symbiotic relationship, the material voice being shaped by my own temporal and spatial influence too.

And there is always a third agent at work: the One that moves through all and imbues each creature to give witness to life and to warn of death.

7

When Man and Woman were Soil: A Latin American Decolonial and Intercultural Perspective on Creation, Spirituality and Environment Grief

MARÍA ALEJANDRA ANDRADE VINUEZA

The Mayan indigenous people say that
in the beginning Kucumatz,
who is the father and mother of humanity,
made man out of clay,
but the rain came and diluted him.
Then he made the man out of wood,
but lightning came and burned him.
In the end, Kucumatz took the sweet corn (Xilot),
ground it and shaped it and made the human couple.
(taken from Popol Vu, Mayan sacred book)

In the beginning, human beings were one with nature. They knew that they and the earth were creatures of the same almighty Creator: they both received his breath of life and they both carried the same divine print in their DNA. They walked in the same soil, ate the same fruits that the land provided, navigated the same seas and drank the same water. They organized their lives around the same seasons and cycles of the moon. They were washed by the same rain, heated by the same sun and sheltered under the same stars. Human beings knew that, just as every animal, they were dust and to dust they would return (Genesis 3.19).

Then the LORD God formed a man from the dust of the ground and breathed into his nostrils the breath of life, and the man became a living being.

Now the LORD God had planted a garden in the east, in Eden; and there he put the man he had formed … He brought them to the man to see what he would name them; and whatever the man called each living creature, that was its name. So the man gave names to all the livestock, the birds in the sky and all the wild animals. (Genesis 2.7–8, 19–20, NIV)

In the beginning, human beings were deeply aware of their interconnectedness and interdependence with all creation: they understood that their own survival and thriving as a species depended directly on the survival and thriving of every animal, plant, river, mountain, insect, bird and tree. The Creator's vision for his creation was one of life in harmonious and loving relationships: between self and God, with oneself, between self and others, and between self and nature. 'The LORD God took the man and put him in the Garden of Eden to work it and *take care of it*' (Genesis 2.15, NIV, my emphasis).

They did not attempt to possess and dominate, as they knew that they were not 'owners' of the other living creatures. This state of mutual, loving relationships with everyone and everything is the essence of what Christina Puchalski defines as 'spirituality', and has been a constant quest for humans:

> Spirituality is the aspect of humanity that refers to the way individuals seek and express meaning and purpose and the way they experience their connectedness to the moment, to self, to others, to nature, and to the significant or sacred.[1]

In the case of indigenous peoples, spirituality permeates their way of life, including their social relationships, their daily practices and their relationship with nature. For many centuries,

---

1 Christina Puchalski et al., 2014, 'Improving the Spiritual Dimension of Whole Person Care: Reaching National and International Consensus', *Journal of Palliative Medicine* 17(6), pp. 642–56.

indigenous communities throughout *Abya Yala*[2] (Latin American continent's name before the Spanish conquest, which has become a symbol of resistance, identity and recognition of the roots and presence of indigenous peoples in the region) have embraced this strong spirit of interconnectedness and interdependence expressed in the biblical text, as well as in Puchalski's definition of spirituality. This sense of 'holistic spirituality' has guided the relationship not only between human beings and transcendence, but also between them, nature and all the community members.

In Andean indigenous communities, the concepts of *Sumak Kawsay* (good living) and *Sumak Qamaña* (good togetherness) express this sense of interconnectedness and interdependence among human beings and with nature. They refer to the responsibility of carrying and nurturing life: our own life, other people's life and the life of *Pachamama* (Mother Earth). Among *kichwa* indigenous communities in Ecuador, *Sumak Kawsay* denotes the idea of a life that does not seek to be 'the very best', or 'better' than other people's lives; it is a life that is 'good enough', a 'satisfactory' life. The concept of *Sumak Qamaña*, on the other side, comes from *Aymara* indigenous communities in Bolivia, and adds the dimension of community: life needs to be 'good' and 'harmonious' for all people in society.[3]

Stories, rites and narratives of daily life are privileged vehicles to preserve and perpetuate this essential sense of coexistence from generation to generation. The Guna people, who inhabit Colombia and Panama, have a meaningful rite around birth, which affirms the extent to which every new human life is deeply connected with God, with his/her community, and with nature:

For the *Gunadule* people, the definition of spirituality can be found in their theological treaty, the *Bad Igala* – 'God's way'.

2 *Abya Yala*, in the Guna language, means 'land in its full maturity' or 'land of vital blood'.

3 Noemi Villaverde Maza, 2015, 'Sumak Kawsay y Sumak Qamaña', *MITO Revista Cultural*, available from http://revistamito.com/sumak-kawsay-y-suma-qamana/, accessed 25/07/20.

For them, spirituality is expressed in the harmony that exists in their relationships: 1) With God – *Baba and Nana* – who has both masculine and feminine characteristics; 2) With the land – *Nabgwana* – and 3) With human beings. *Gunadule* spirituality is nourished by rites and ceremonies that seek to connect people with each other and with nature. The first ceremony of every individual is called 'My first tree' and is performed at birth: when a girl or boy are born, the midwife delivers the umbilical cord with the placenta to the father or companion. They sow the umbilical cord and the placenta, along with a seed that symbolizes life (like a banana or a cocoa seed). From that day on, every time that a member of the community passes by the tree, he/she has the responsibility to take care of it: with good words, gestures, pouring water on it. In this way, the connection of the individual with others, with the nature and with the Giver of life is expressed in very concrete ways, from the beginning of life. When the fruit grows – be it a banana, cocoa, another fruit tree – and the harvest time arrives, the fruit of the tree is prepared in a juice and shared with all the boys and girls, so that they all drink this germinal drink – it is the special ceremony of the new community member. With this ceremony, the *Gunadule* people thank God for the life, thank the land for the fruit, celebrate the fertility of women, connect with the community and recognize that all are interconnected and interdependent.[4]

In the beginning, human beings were one with nature. They were soil. They were interconnected. They knew that they depended on each other. This is what the Creator of the world created. This is how it was supposed to be. Then, something happened which broke this fragile balance. For the indigenous inhabitants of *Abya Yala* evil came from the Eastern seas; Spanish caravels full of swords, Bibles and greed. Colonialism brought death and the exploitation of people and nature. Indigenous populations – who knew the living world much more intimately than any doctor or scientist coming from the 'Old World' – were called 'savages', 'barbarians' and 'uncivilized'. They were considered

4 Interview with Jocabed Solano, a Guna theologian, September 2019.

soulless and, therefore, inferior beings, close to animals. Modernity – the other side of colonialism's coin – imposed a eurocentric understanding of being, knowing and believing, which became the model. The cycles of the sun and the moon were replaced by the rhythms of consumption and trade. The 'common good' and 'good enough' were replaced by indiscriminate exploitation, individualism and unlimited ambition. The *Pachamama*, with all her abundance, suffered the consequences of human greed: her trees – her arms – were cut; her soil – her flesh – was perforated; her minerals – her organs – were extracted; her rivers – her veins – were polluted. Creation, as a living being, 'has been groaning as in the pains of childbirth right up to the present time' (Romans 8.22, NIV). In Latin America and the Caribbean, the impact of colonialism and modernity is present today in the damage to the environment but also in the damage between people. This is the bigger environmental crisis of all times, generated by the only living species that is capable of destroying itself.

A theological explanation to this crisis can be found in Genesis 3, when human beings tried to be equal to God. This passage from the sacred book makes it clear that the relationship with God is not the only one that got damaged (v. 8); the relationships with self (v. 10), with others (v. 12) and with nature (vv. 15, 17) also broke that day. The interdependent spirituality of human creatures disintegrated and, as a result, all its relationships – with God, with self, with others and with the rest of creation – were distorted. This distortion, among other things, makes us unable to see the Creator's footprint in everything and everyone, including ourselves. It becomes easy to sell, buy, violate and exploit. Poverty, corruption, racism, xenophobia, violence, injustice and the exploitation and destruction of our 'Common House' are symptoms of this real crisis: a crisis of a broken spirituality. Colossians 1.15–20 narrates God's response to that crisis: Jesus interrupted history 'to reconcile to himself all things, whether things on earth or things in heaven, by making peace through his blood, shed on the cross' (Colossians 1.20, NIV).

Can our wounded spirituality be truly healed now?

Understanding that the current environmental crisis is the result of broken, disconnected relationships helps to understand that, unless this root cause is redeemed, every well-intentioned action will never be enough. In other words, if the problem deals with spirituality, disconnectedness and lack of meaning, then the solution deals with healing our wounded spirituality. The reconstruction of spirituality is such a profound issue that there are no shortcuts to remedy it: it is not about patching up problems to feel less guilty and satisfy the ego. A truly spiritual restoration is needed to reconnect human beings with everything, including the environment. But, because the wound is so deep, renewal will not come easily, nor quickly; it will require giving true space to grief and lament.

Lament is not a popular practice within many modern and postmodern societies. Often it is quite the opposite, as sentiments of hope and victory make people feel much better. A dominant capitalist culture does not help either; grief competes with empty narratives of (sometimes fake) success. This is not the case in many indigenous traditions in *Abya Yala* who conceive and embrace grief as an integral part of life. Lament allows them to keep on track and find the way when it is lost. In similar ways, some Christian traditions have embraced grief and death as unavoidable aspects of Christian life. Images like dying to the old self (Romans 6.6) or the wheat seed that needs to die in order to come to life and bring fruit (John 12.24) have helped Christians throughout history to avoid the temptation of running away from grief and, instead, give it enough space to restore and give life. A spirit of lament is where we must begin if we are to step towards healing.

The first step is recognizing and naming the damage that human creatures have made to their environments. It is about seeing, observing, listening attentively, without giving explanations, reasons and excuses; in a non-defensive way. It is a space to acknowledge the pain and destruction that human beings have done to every other species, but it is also the space to take responsibility for the part that 'We' – 'I' – have played in that destruction. It is moving from the impersonal 'they' to the responsible 'I'. It is about looking at 'my' own thoughts, attitudes, behaviours and life choices that contribute to kill the 'Common House' we live in. It is also acknowledging that, as my theology and beliefs shape my actions, I need to question them if they prevent me from preserving life in all its forms.

The second step comes from the first and deals with giving a space to address pain properly. This step builds on the capacity to 'listen and observe' but adds the capacity to 'feel'. It is about 'seeing with the heart' – *corazonar*, a Spanish term used by decolonial anthropologists to stress the need to build knowledge from a warm 'insurgent' wisdom.[5] Once the effects of environmental justice are evident, we must feel the pain that has been caused to every living creature: to sea animals, birds, trees, seas, forests, land …

The third step relates to giving a true space for grief and lament, in respectful silence or in cries of despair. Grief and lament can be individual, but they also need to be collective, as the destruction to the environment is caused by both individual actions, individual sins – as well as collective actions – structural, social sin.

This leads to the fourth step: true repentance, which is not cheap remorse but rather a healthy sentiment of guilt. Repentance is the turning point that marks a difference between past and present. Genuine repentance provides the strength needed to walk through the fifth step.

The fifth step is radical change and restitution, as no sustainable and life-giving change will ever come about without a spirit of restorative justice. It is not about light – superficial – changes; it is about a deep conversion of behaviours, attitudes and lifestyles that emerge from a true awareness and desire to reconnect.

Finally, the sixth step is restoring forgiveness, without which the process would not be complete. The capacity of nature to regenerate is a gift of grace: it keeps hope alive and reminds us that God's forgiveness is always available when there is true repentance and commitment to life.

---

5 Patricio Guerrero Arias, 2012, 'Corazonar desde el calor de las sabidurías insurgentes, la frialdad de la teoría y la metodología / Corazonar from insurgent's wisdoms warm, the coldness of theory and the methodology', *Sophía* (13), available from www.researchgate.net/publication/318613751_Cora zonar_desde_el_calor_de_las_sabidurias_insurgentes_la_frialdad_de_la_ teoria_y_la_metodologia_Corazonar_from_insurgents'_wisdoms_warm_ the_coldness_of_the_theory_and_the_methodology, accessed 25/07/20.

Christian and *Gunadule* theologies are closer than what we think. They both understand creation as a sacred action that transcends human beings and is cosmic in scale. The Psalmist expressed it well:

> The heavens declare the glory of God;
>> the skies proclaim the work of his hands.
>
> Day after day they pour forth speech;
>> night after night they reveal knowledge.
>
> They have no speech, they use no words;
>> no sound is heard from them.
>
> Yet their voice goes out into all the earth,
>> their words to the ends of the world.
>
> In the heavens God has pitched a tent for the sun.
>> It is like a bridegroom coming out of his chamber,
>> like a champion rejoicing to run his course.
>
> It rises at one end of the heavens
>> and makes its circuit to the other;
>> nothing is deprived of its warmth.
>
> (Psalm 19.1–6, NIV)

Furthermore, God's communitarian essence – the Trinity in Christian theology and *BabaNana* in *Gunadule* theology – affirm the desire for creation to live in loving relationship with God, self, others and the entire creation: a 'cosmic harmony'. Interdependence and interconnectedness are the definitions of a vibrant and healthy spirituality. When human beings broke their relationship with God, all the other relationships broke up too, creating a 'cosmic imbalance'. Pollution, exploitation and destruction of the environment can be understood as symptoms of a deeper crisis: a crisis of spirituality, resulting from broken relationships, disconnection and lack of purpose.

Our injured spirituality needs to be healed, and this healing process is not meant to be easy; it requires intentionality in seeing, feeling, lamenting, repenting, changing and healing. If our brokenness has created an imbalanced relationship with all the living beings with whom we share our 'Big House', then embrac-

ing lament is a necessary step to restore the lost balance, heal our
wounded spirituality and believe again in the prophet's vision:

> A day will come when the wolf will live peacefully beside
>   the wobbly-kneed lamb,
> and the leopard will lie down with the young goat;
> The calf and yearling, newborn and slow, will rest secure
>   with the lion;
> and a little child will tend them all.
> Bears will graze with the cows they used to attack;
>   even their young will rest together,
>   and the lion will eat hay, like gentle oxen.
> Neither will a baby who plays next to a cobra's hole
>   nor a toddler who sticks his hand into a nest of vipers
>   suffer harm.
> All my holy mountain will be free of anything hurtful
>   or destructive,
>   for as the waters fill the sea,
> The entire earth will be filled with the knowledge of
>   the Eternal.
> (Isaiah 11.6–9, *The Voice*)

8

Failing Mandela

PETER FOX AND MILES GILJAM

Our consumer society is busy killing our planet. We are killers. But we also grieve the loss of life we are guilty of ending. How can we grieve well in these tragic circumstances? How can our grief catalyse awareness, hope and action? The white South African community, in which both authors grew up, has grappled for years with its role in the creation of the evil systems of colonialism and apartheid. We examine South Africa's recent history, through the lens of an unfinished grief process, to see how people from the so-called developed world, involved in the environmental movement, can learn from our community.

My name is Peter Fox. I was shaped by the fraught years of the 1970s and 80s of apartheid South Africa. I grew up in segregated apartheid society and served as a church minister in the all-white suburbs. I was involved with white anti-apartheid faith leaders, like the Revd Beyers Naude. They persuaded me to act in civil disobedience against apartheid laws. Sadly, we were in a minority in our community. In the 1980s, during the endgame of apartheid, I facilitated groups for the National Initiative for Reconciliation (NIR). I remember hearing the stories of an Afrikaner Dominee whose grandmother was interned in a British concentration camp after land, property and life was taken, by my people, during the South African War. That meeting took place in a black township. At another meeting, in a wealthy white suburb, we heard the story of torture and imprisonment of black detainees suspected of subversive activities. They would be arrested without trial while their families had no access to them in prison. Together we felt each other's pain and mourned what our society had done to us. But only a small group of white leaders had the courage and opportunity to step into these spaces of pain and truth. For those who did, we faced an awakening where we discovered to grieve injustice is to face the pain, name the feelings and engage what the loss means. Only then can a measure of healing of the wound begin. Through the work of the churches, enough of our political elite were able to experience this process, which contributed to the miraculous coming together of enemies to negotiate a new South Africa, the Rainbow Nation, in the 1990s.

My name is Miles Giljam. I am a child, and citizen, of the Rainbow Nation of Nelson Mandela and Desmond Tutu. But the Rainbow Nation is dead. I grew up in the heady rollercoaster transition years of 1990s South Africa. Over five years our leaders negotiated our way into miracle nation status. Miracle nation. Magical nation. Magical thinking?

I became the first generation of Rainbow Nation citizens, coming together around a new South African narrative of togetherness and forgiveness, designed to overcome the past. Those early years were fantastic. We built interracial friendships, socialized in one another's neighbourhoods, learnt to dance to different types of music. Our lives changed and we changed. However, at a deeper level very little changed. While we enjoyed exploring this new world, the Truth and Reconciliation Commission (TRC) was exposing the truth of the apartheid system and the crimes against humanity that sustained it. The reality is that very few white people paid attention. Many opposed it or didn't testify. Too frightened to face the great evil they had helped perpetrate, our elders didn't listen to the pain. We moved on largely unchanged.

Twenty years later we discovered that the Rainbow Nation was dead. We had followed a path of unhealthy grieving. Our white elders demonstrated denial, avoidance and rationalization. My generation indulged in magical thinking, desperately working to become 'good whites', hoping that changed narratives, and surface behaviour transformation, would be enough to change our nation. This took us down false paths to solve the issues that faced us. Magical thinking. Magical nation. Miracle nation? Our unhealthy grieving meant we didn't give ourselves a chance to shift the underlying structural injustice.

Choosing healthy grieving for the planet

Grief, if managed well, is a profoundly transformative emotion. If we are able to grieve properly the process challenges and changes our identity. We become someone different. Healthy grieving may be the tool by which we refashion the priorities and rhythms of our society to deal with our new reality of environmental collapse.

Grieving is a complicated roller-coaster ride of new beginnings and old endings. It needs spaces for silence, solitude, reflection, contemplation and mindful awareness. It involves an attitude of curiosity and humility in understanding the story of the other. Healthy grieving will facilitate new expressions of hope and action. But such an assignment is hard; and especially hard if you are culpable in causing the death you grieve.

The danger is that, like white South Africans, developed-world environmentalists overcome by loss and guilt will give into the temptation of unhealthy grieving. They could be stuck in apathy and anger, like older white South Africans: consumed by a narcissistic grief focused on the personal loss of privilege, as they see the disappearance of the natural world they love. Or, like Miles' youthful 1994 generation, they could embrace a grief-avoiding magical-thinking narrative, allied with some personal lifestyle change, that they vainly hope will save the earth. This is especially dangerous as the environmental movement shifts in scale, from a small group of dedicated sacrificial activists to a younger mainstream movement. There is no such thing as a 'good white', a 'good environmentalist' or a 'good consumer' – unless the system that provides our power, and oppresses people and planet, is profoundly transformed. The magical narrative may offer personal salvation for a time, but the cycle of violence will continue into the next generation.

In South Africa the new generation has become disillusioned. Young black activists have thrown away the entire Rainbow Nation narrative. They express the pain of the unimaginable losses of 400 years of oppression. They have called Mandela a sell-out, pointing to the fact that little has changed economically in 20 years. Our system of oppression is still intact and the cycle of violence and pain is still turning. But Mandela wasn't a sell-out – there were too many white South Africans who didn't have the courage to respond to his leadership and to truly grieve. We didn't listen to the stories and pain at the TRC, or build authentic relationships across the colour line. We didn't fundamentally change our systems of oppression. We didn't break the cycle.

The developed-world environmental movement needs to understand that they are part of the system that caused the climate problem. Only by truly confronting the pain they have caused as perpetrators will they experience authentic grief that brings hope and deep change. We cannot afford to leave this work to the next generation. The planet won't survive another cycle of violence and pain. Bewilderment and rage will write the agenda, blocking the shift to new ways that serve the well-being of all.

Listening

An authentic grieving process listens to the pain and despair of others. In South Africa we lacked the courage to truly listen. Only through living in proximity to those oppressed by poverty and violence, like Jesus did, will we be able to build relationships. The experience of truly listening will challenge us; disrupt our thinking; undermine our identity; remove our sense of righteousness; dislodge our egos; undermine our power. It is exhausting and you will want to run away at every moment. It is easier to retreat to our place of familiar safety. We must face the demons and dark that will devour us if we ignore them or spiritualize them away.

But the language of pain and loss is usually hard to understand. It comes from a deep groaning within, and it is almost never in the language of the powerful. Are we able to listen equally to the eloquent argument, the cry of pain or the burning of a building? When we listen to our damaged planet can we deliberately choose proximity to the depressing places where nature is damaged and dying, rather than the few pristine pockets of life where we so often gain happiness? Are we able to listen to the drought and the hurricane, or contemplate, with all our senses, the river overflowing with sewage?

As we listen, exposed to death and brokenness, we will feel anger, despair, frustration and rage. If we face these hard emotions, letting them pass through us as a rupturing reality, we may become vulnerable witnesses, able to heal wounds and emerge into a new identity. We must expose ourselves to death in order that God may bring life again. This will be painful. Only then can we repent.

Lament and repentance

Authentic mourning bridges the divide between our self-deceiving storylines and the harsh reality that confronts us in our pain. We must lament and confess our complicity in systems of economic and social evil and the damage this has done to people and nature. Our grief journey must acknowledge, deep in our own hearts, the repentance that is needed. King David, exposed in his unjust behaviour, phrases this so powerfully in the psalms: 'Have mercy, O God. Cast me not away from your Presence. Deliver me from the guilt of bloodshed. Teach me wisdom in my secret place. Create in me a clean heart' (Psalm 51, paraphrased).

Grieving means no longer hiding behind facades of respectability and ideology. Grief challenges us, empties us, breaks us. Our response needs to be to seek the blessing David petitions for: 'The sacrifice, you require, O God, is a broken spirit and a contrite heart. That you will not despise.'

Don't hide behind clever analysis and theories – feel the pain, own the loss and allow the Spirit to awaken new hope. Wait for the Spirit to give new life. South African whites didn't hold the pain for long enough that it would truly break us and empty us, so our hearts could be changed. Consequently we have an unfinished reconciliation project.

Resurrection and reparation

Grief is ultimately not an individual pursuit. Only by grieving in community, in proximity, can the perpetrators be healed and transformed, and victims empowered. Black South Africans taught us this through the love and forgiveness inherent in *ubuntu*. But we didn't reciprocate appropriately. Authentic grieving doesn't lead to depression and apathy – it invites a focused attention to the pain of others, creates dialogue and allows us to access together a new humanity that embraces failure, arrogance and entitlement. All our stories become important. As we respond to the climate crisis, our community is broadened to the whole of creation, of which humans are a small but exquisite part. Together we can make choices that breathe hope for a different future and position us for a new resurrection identity. In courage and community we can emerge slowly into the sun.

The 1994 South African transition was an elite project. A small group of powerful white leaders, forced to the negotiation table and acting out of self-interest, briefly connected with some of the pain of the black majority, allowing them to remove their hurdles to liberation. But the elite, both white and black, quickly became separated, in their comfortable homes and offices, from the pain and grief of the ordinary person. Elites have the resources to insulate themselves from pain. They can avoid the process of mourning and transformation.

To reimagine our world effectively we cannot rely on the developed world, our global elite, to make good choices for us. Their solutions will protect the same system that damages the environment and nurtures their current way of life. This work will not be led by the elites. And if you are reading this you are probably part of an elite! The solutions will be found by those who are living in closest proximity to the pain of the earth and are the most politically and economically marginalized. Our role as members of the elite, benefiting from the consumer economy, is to find the strength to shift systems and institutions so that direct power is returned to the hands of those in closest proximity to pain. These new institutions need to be reparative, honouring the capacity for local leaders to implement sustainable change.

The Christian pilgrimage does not end in pain. Every death holds with it the promise of a resurrection. Creation constantly regenerates. This change, however, comes at great cost. It requires us to die to our old ways and embrace a simpler life, in solidarity with the oppressed, alongside those who demand a just and sustainable economic transformation. Are you willing to feel the pain and allow your grief to change you and the world around you? Will you embrace the sacrifice of a broken spirit and a contrite heart? It's a sacrifice many white South Africans were unable to make in 1994. We hope it's a sacrifice that we can all make now as we face the climate crisis.

9

Learning from Irular Laments

BHARADHYDASAN KANNAN

The Irular, meaning 'dark' in Tamil, have a strange connection to some of the world's most venomous snakes. The tribe is renowned for their ability to trap snakes and harvest venom for antidotes that have saved countless lives in India, although they are much more than snake charmers. Their ethnomedical knowledge is legendary and has proved to be an effective remedy for several maladies. They have a distinct linguistic identity with a defined set of sociopolitical divisions that further branches out into clans and subclans. Irulars are listed as 'Particularly Vulnerable Tribal Groups' by the government of India and are now spread across all the southern states of India, mainly concentrated around the Western Ghats adjoining Tamil Nadu and Kerala. They are accorded the lowest in the tribal hierarchy. Their belief systems revolve around the divinity of tigers, cats, ant mounds and traditional Hindu pantheons. They were primarily a hunting and gathering community, with agrarian activity limited to the 'slash and burn' agricultural technique. Increased legislation and sensitivity towards wildlife conservation deemed many of their traditional practices unlawful. What followed after the embargo was a vicious circle of slavery and discrimination based on caste and identity, despite anti-discriminative legislation. It also set in motion the migration of Irulars throughout Tamil Nadu and Kerala looking for better employment.

Irulars and their heritage have considerable cultural influence in Pondicherry, a former French colony on the eastern coast of India. Villivakkam, an important part of Pondicherry, was named after an Irular subclan, although this may seem implausible to native hearers because of the sociopolitical exploitation that Irulars are subjected to in the region. The city of Coimbatore, fondly called the 'Manchester of South India' owing to its sprawling textile and heavy electrical industry, is named after an Irular warrior 'Koyan'. I was fortunate to spend time with some Irulars living in Pondicherry. They are hard-working, shy, and zealous about their tribal and community identity. Most men were working as agricultural labourers and women as domestic help, and their younger people were interested in education and sports. They have historically been ignored in the official census of India and the government did not accord them 'Scheduled Tribe'[1] status. The status was finally accorded in the year 2016 under pressure from academics, social activists and historians. Despite these measures, they still suffer from poverty, lack of access to clean drinking water and electricity, prevalent bad living conditions, and discrimination in the workplace. They continue to consume rats as a source of protein and are largely disconnected from their traditional snake-trapping practices, citing lack of a conducive ecosystem and animal protective laws.

Their tryst with Christianity began with the arrival of Europeans in the Nilgiri region. The Nilgiris are a vivid palette of lush mountains, named 'Nil-Giri', meaning 'blue mountain' in Tamil. The climatic and geographical isolation presented a 'concealing blanket' for the tribes, helping them thrive against waves of cultural and political invasions. Nilgiri is the traditional home of five native tribes: Badaga, Irula, Toda, Kota and Kurumbas. The famous 5,000-year-old rock painting at Kil Kotagiri is rightfully asserted as cultural heritage by the Irular tribe. The symbols bore resemblance to Indus script, signifying both ancient tradition and the importance of their hunting culture. But the presence of tribal groups with distinct languages, customs and social orders, along with the diverse ecosystem of Nilgiri, made the destination a hotspot of anthropological curiosity under British colonial rule. The British also realized the region's economic importance and began the industrialization process, mainly through the labour of tribal groups. The Nilgiri Biosphere Reserves, earmarked in 1986, boasted rare wildlife and thriving biodiversity, including 3,300

---

1 The status testifies to the marginalized state of their community and helps them access affirmative action programmes.

species of flowers. While Nilgiri's climate attracted tea cultivation for the East India Company, its scenic beauty, biodiversity and tribal heritage appealed to anthropologists, historians, linguists and naturalists. The region became a hub of education, industry, tourism and political mobilization, soon transforming into the informal capital city of Colonial Madras Presidency during summer.

Loss of homeland in Nilgiris

Tribal societies posed stiff resistance to the expansionist policy of the East India Company. This anger was also expressed in opposing Christianity and its messengers: the missionaries. The Santhal rebellion in North India was one such reaction to the influx of non-tribals into the tribal ecosystem. The Santhals were peace-loving nomadic tribes subjected to migration by the British to employ them in clearing forest tracts and hunt animals. The displaced tribals were forced into harsh labour and a ruthless usury system that cost them their land and freedom. The credit, if unpaid, demanded the tribe to become slaves of Zamindars (landlords), Mahajans (Brahmin/bankers). Discontent gradually grew against the local feudal system and reached its peak when the British government introduced a new land bill called the '1793 Permanent Settlement Act'. The bill gave non-tribals (mainly the Mahajans and landlords) permission to usurp tribal land. By contrast, missionary education played an important part in raising political education, and tribals became increasingly aware of their political and social rights. The Santhal rebellion came to an end after a brutal suppression, massacring thousands of tribe members. Scottish historian William Wilson Hunter described the fateful confrontation in the following words:

> It was not warring; they did not understand yielding. As long as their national drum beat, the whole party would stand, and allow themselves to be shot down. Their arrows often killed our men, and so we had to fire on them as long as they stood. When their drum ceased, they would move off a quarter of a

mile; then their drums beat again, and they calmly stood till we came up and poured a few volleys into them. There was not a sepoy in the war who did not feel ashamed of himself.

The Santhal rebellion sent waves across the Indian subcontinent and inspired dialogues criticizing British imperialism. The aftermath of the Santhal rebellion brought the Munda tribe into their quest for freedom and self-government. Birsa Munda, a young rebel who was christened as David Birsa Munda, renounced his new-found faith to oppose British-sponsored land reforms that allowed 'outsiders' to lay claim to tribal areas. Educated in a German missionary school, he led an armed rebellion and even initiated his new religion. This marked a new chapter in tribal resistance against British and local feudalism: Birsa used simple songs to propagate his message on the land assertion, rooted in their ancestral ties with nature. This movement inspired other uprisings across the nation. The Munda rebellion ended in 1900 with the custodial death of Birsa Munda at the young age of 21; the rebellion pushed British administration to reform its policies towards tribal areas. As a result, the Chotanagpur Tenant Act was passed in 1908. The Act asserted the rights of tribes over their land and prohibited transferring land to non-tribal entities.

Similar disturbances were witnessed in the Nilgiri tribal belt. Foreign presence in a previously tribal-inhabited region brought conflict over the ecosystem. While tribal beliefs revolved around biotic and abiotic elements of the ecosystem, the new arrivals used it for recreation, with a keen eye on the economic viability of the region's tea and coffee plantations. The Nilgiri tribes considered every aspect of their ecosystem as remnants of their ancestors; Irulars consider themselves descendants of cats. The various gods they revered were associated with nature: Mariamman, the goddess of rain, and Ellaiamman, the goddess who protected their village borders. They practised divination and soothsaying to receive words of assurance from their deity, seeking protection from invaders, disease and bad omens. But new economic ventures in Nilgiri meant the need for cheap labour. The local tribes had previously taken what they needed from the forests. The advancing deforestation and internal displacement forced members of the tribes to look for employment in newly created cash crop plantations. The influx of immigrants from the surrounding area into tribal reserves disturbed the ancient harmony of the mountains. Gradually, their land was converted into agricultural and tourist estates wherein tribes enrolled themselves as manual labourers.

Industrialization and urbanization have significantly altered the Irular lifestyle and their interaction with the ecosystem. Illiteracy and isolation are often cited as the main reason for their marginalization. This however is not the case, since tribal identity is itself perceived as something debasing in Indian social consciousness. Their distinct linguistic identity, choice of habitation and dietary habits often come under attack from the Hindu Vegetarian and Caste Puritan groups. The nomadic lives of Irulars were challenged when the British introduced the Criminal Tribe Act in 1871 under which nomadic and certain tribes were considered habitual criminals. This restricted their mobility and altered their outlook towards their nomadic lifestyle and profession. The subsequent legislation on the protection of wild animals banned hunting of certain animals, which affected the livelihood of Irulars. These situations set in motion the displacement of Irulars from the Nilgiris and their migration across southern states. The migrating Irulars often fall into the web of unemployment and social exclusion, leading to impoverishment and loss of identity. Irulars are still found predominantly in Nilgiris but exhibit a poor health index and a marginalized socio-economic state.

The lamentations of Irulars

Irulars maintain a strong community bond, using festivals and social gatherings to showcase their ancestral arts to the younger generations. Traditional Irular songs revolved around their agricultural practices and veneration of their deities. Irulars of Pondicherry place special emphasis on Kannimar songs, dedicated to the seven deities. The deity song also called 'Pey Pattu' describes their deities and exalts nature's elements. It speaks of the beauty surrounding the flowers, birds, trees, shrubs and herbs. The songs contain traces of lost biotic elements that Irulars cherished, and the imagery is slowly getting replaced with mainstream elements and influence from popular culture.

Irular songs are also an important medium for expressing grief over the loss of traditional homes as a result of migration and unemployment. Irulars in urban spaces are slowly losing their varied forms of verbal arts. Traditional Irular musicology contained riddles, myths, folklores, struggles against dominant tribes, and moral anecdotes that were passed through generations. Irulars living in Pondicherry have infused their ancient religious beliefs with contemporary music yet retained their native tongue. Their most popular song gives an introduction to Irular identity and the place they belong, containing vivid details of their landscape, the animals, birds, the challenges they faced. This song is often recited by Irular children when confirming their identities before the government officials to receive caste certificates. This form of humiliation is still prevalent, and authorities claim to have no other way of identifying Irulars. This incident is also mentioned in one of their songs portraying the ordeal they go through to access social welfare programmes.

Strikingly, the history-telling in their songs includes the preservation of the natural ecosystem to which Irulars tie their existence:

இயற்கையோடு வாழ்கிறோம்,
(Iyarkayodu Vazhgirom)

மரம் வெட்டி பிழைக்கிறோம்,
(Maram Vetti Pizhaikirom)

செங்கல் சூளையில் உழைக்கிறோம்,
(Sengal Sulaiyil Uzhaikirom)

வாழவழி தெரியாம கொத்தடிமையா வாழ்கிறோம்,
(Vaazha Vali Theriyama Kothadimaya Vazhgirom)

காடுகுள்ள தான் எங்கள் வம்சம் வாழுது,
(Kaadukul Than Yengal Vamsam Vazhudhu)

அந்த இயற்கை அழிஞ்சா இருளர் வம்சம் அழியுது.
(Antha Iyarkai Azhinja Irular Vamsam Azhiyidhu)

We lived with nature, and survived using its resources,
Now toiling in brick kilns, reduced to slavery with no means
  for livelihood,
Our tribe lives in the forests,
The Irular tribe will die if forests die.
(Irular song, in Tamil and romanized script)

Irular songs document the deforestation Nilgiris underwent
during the colonial rule; a popular song describes the felling of
trees for the construction of a cotton mill in Coimbatore. Their
folklore speaks of Irular heroes using forest cover as protective
shields against intruders. Their songs inform younger generations
of their struggles and the need to conserve the forests, creating
awareness against environmental degradation, bonded slavery
and social exploitations attached to tribal identity. The songs
also reflect their reverence towards animals and often address
animals with honorific titles like 'rasa' for elephants, meaning
'king' in the Irular language. More importantly, their songs
encapsulate the suffering of Irulars and their position in a
caste-ridden society. The insertion of Tamil words in their songs
also denotes the dying Irular language, which is scriptless and
gradually losing significance. The marginalization of Irulars is
a direct consequence of breaching their homeland and refusing
their rightful assertion over the forest and its resources. Irulars in
Cuddalore were terribly affected by the tsunami in 2004, but the
damage to their hamlet was contained because of the mangroves
blanketing their village. This incident reinstated their belief in the
ecosystem as the protector of their tribe.

Christian guilt and learning from Irular grief

I have been touched by sermons in Tamil churches that describe
grief over their failure to continue the mission of St Thomas,
the ancient apostle to India. The churches in Tamil Nadu held

themselves responsible for not bringing the revival the disciple intended. But what they fail to understand is the necessity for caste and identity discourse in the gospel. The Church of St Thomas mainly consists of upper castes. This has usurped the disciple's mission and played a greater role in diluting the gospel and tolerating divisions based on birth. The tribal belt in north India is mainly served by Tamil church bodies, but they largely shy away from discussing 'identities' and assume the non-existence of marginalization. The impact of missionaries from the colonial period was significant in establishing these institutions, and their effects are still felt today. Catholic churches across Tamil Nadu have now adopted the practice of 'ecological offerings' to God, seen as a parallel for tribal or agrarian customs. However, the question of tribal identity and ecological conservation remains largely ignored.

My experience with the Irulars has changed my understanding of the mission of the Church. The most important realization was the tribal quest for acceptance without needing to change their social, sartorial and dietary customs. There is also a need to instate debates and discussion surrounding identities and castes that Indian churches mostly shy away from. I have learned to read the Bible in the context of diverse identities encompassing their ecological systems. From Noah's ark to the fish in the book of Jonah, ecology has always been integral in the conversation between humans and God.

Irulars are facing an immediate crisis, prevented from accessing nature by those who say that these restrictions will save the forests. These are the same people who also develop cash-crop agriculture, industrialization and tea plantations. Prolonged industrialization and foreign presence in the Nilgiris have triggered eco-anxiety among tribes who have played no part in the degradation process. And yet I have witnessed many Christians turning a blind eye to environmental degradation, believing that the 'End Days' will contain such catastrophes, and climate change is just a part of the final episode.

Irulars present us with the reality of ecology loss and the consequences of uprooting people from a cherished homeland. Irulars are not only grieving the loss of home but also remain silenced spectators of the degradation done to their former home. Their songs and folklores are their expression of grief, and these laments can teach the Church to listen to the tribal claim to their land, giving new meaning to God's assurance of provision for a promised land both on earth and in the kingdom to come. Their songs have an important message for the Church, both in repenting for the past and in understanding the present: we are not solely individual beings, but we need to live in community with the God-created world. The places we belong matter to us, because they matter to God.

The Edge of the World

CALEB GORDON

My family has not been in Alaska as long as the Native tribes or the Russian villages. But they've been there since before there were paved roads or grocery stores. When my great-grandfather arrived in the 1930s, it was not yet a US state but a 'territory', and there was little in the way of infrastructure. Most journeys of any significant distance required boats, and the arrival of supplies and comforts were forecast in weeks and months. This was at a time when the new technologies of 'modern life' were just beginning to emerge in full force as an American institution – televisions and telephones, fast cars and department store catalogues – and yet my great-grandfather headed up north, to a wild, largely uninhabited land to build a life there in the wilderness. As it's been told to me, he visited once and found his health greatly improved by the cool, dry air. He couldn't shake off the idea of creating something for himself after returning home, and moved up for good a short time later. It's not as though my family have been anti-technology purists, though; it wasn't about rejecting a modern way of life, at least not entirely. I think it was more the call of the mountains and the sea, and wanting to be close to them. Not rejection of the former nearly so much as attraction to the latter. And wanting to build a way of life that was between themselves and God, and maybe not so much to do with the rest of the world. An impossible ambition, perhaps.

My grandparents can recall a time when their nearest neighbour was a point of light in the dark, represented by the barely visible glow of an oil lantern from the next cabin over, a mile or two down the long hillside. And even now, it's still relatively easy, compared to the rest of the world, to find places in Alaska where there aren't any artificial lights, and the air is dry and clear. Looking up on a winter night is an easy reminder that you're a tiny creature on a modest but hospitable planet. I've been in places so cold and clear and dark that it's impossible not to feel in your bones that the cold is not just 'cold' – it's *space*; it's the sensation of touching the void as a mortal creature. Somehow the purity of the darkness and vibrancy of its celestial textures forces a reinterpretation of 'cold' as more meaningful than the moisture in your nose turning brittle, or as a spasm of nerves releasing a wave of bumps across your skin. It's difficult to describe what it *feels like* to be separated from the sun, to be as close to the stars as possible without leaving the planet. Being so close to that boundary is something that has always made me feel closer to God. Not because I don't think God is near, but because I think God is also far, and a clear winter night on the edge of the planet is as far as you can ever see with your own eyes.

When I am in wild places, I feel something very similar to looking up at the stars. A daylight version, you might say. Again it's the matter of looking out from my own world and into another, one that I have not made, one that has not been constructed by people. It used to be that people would go into this other world, the world outside of safety and the known, to find food, materials and sometimes solitude and reflection. Growing up I was taught to see wilderness as vast, beautiful and brimming with sustenance. I was also taught to see, in the mountains and forests and rivers and seas, in their colours and powers and heights, the beauty and majesty of God. To see in them a sign and testament to their creator, to *my* creator. Nowhere else have I been where the transition from civilization to wilderness is so abrupt and so profound. It is as though you are passing between worlds. It's hard to overstate how much I value the possibility of that passage, and how much it pains me to see it diminished, blurred, retreating.

There is still an incredible amount of uninhabited land in Alaska, but attitudes and activities continue to change, and to change *it*. Or perhaps the attitudes haven't changed as much as I imagine, and time simply presses on in its relentlessly complicating subtractions, while we continue to reveal to ourselves what we've always been. In summer, roads become clogged with recreational vehicles the size of small houses, towing jeeps and trailers and jockeying for position at campsites and riversides. Cheaply built condominiums spring up at scenic locations, 'stimulating the economy' and advertising charming views of fishing villages to out-of-state renters and buyers. There's something that unnerves and saddens me to see a way of life become the scenic backdrop to another – where relation to place becomes a race to purchase land with a view, as an investment in something quickly disappearing. And it disappears faster the scarcer it becomes.

Where most of my family lives, there are still snowy mountains across a glittering bay. But it feels like something arrived with the pioneers – perhaps its full meaning can only be grasped at the distance of a couple of generations – something that lurks, that feeds on beauty, or disregards it, and turns it into something else. I don't suppose it's anything new; I suspect it's something humans have always carried in ourselves. Maybe Alaska is just unique in the sharpness of the image; the speed of the transition over time. Those who live there observe at first hand the cresting wave of modern civilization as it rises past thawing mountains and washes into the last untouched places.

A lot has changed in the last century. A lot has changed since my father was a boy. Journeys that used to take days now require only hours. We don't exist in the same way in the spaces between the places we know. Or rather, we don't know the places between any more. I don't, anyway, not as the older folks do. And the relationship to the land is more ambiguous, too. Where once people lived in a state of vitalizing and tangible dependence, there now exists a kind of hybrid dependence: partially dependent on the land, and partially dependent on everything and everywhere else. I wonder too, sometimes, if this is a similar sort of passage between worlds, and what that means. Are we dependent on hunting and fishing ... or not? Does that sense of dependence facilitate our passage – can it move us nearer or farther to God? It doesn't seem as if we're dependent on the places we know any more, at least in any obvious way. Not dependent on *Alaska*, on the place we tell people we're from.

My father is an avid and expert hunter and my upbringing was punctuated by hunting and fishing trips. It's always been a part of the way that I know Alaska. I also grew up with multiple large department stores mere minutes from my house. Hunting never felt necessary, the way it does for my father, and his father, and his before him. Now the lights of houses have begun to creep down the backs of the ridges that border the old family hunting grounds; rich forests and swamps whose moose sustained multiple generations. There are power lines running across them now, and cellphone and radio towers in a series of spines along the tops of the hills, fitted with blinking lights to be more easily seen by aircraft. There are many trails and many travellers: hunters, tourists, joyriders, escapists. The moose are harder to find, and smaller. Aeroplanes drone across the sky throughout the day, and the irregular buzzing of ATVs has likewise become part of that landscape.

I've killed one moose. I was in my early teens. We spotted it early in the morning with a long-range telescope, a little yearling bull with one deformed antler hanging down behind its eye. It wandered across the valley below us, so we moved down the hill for a closer shot. I raised the rifle, aimed the crosshairs as well as I could, and shot it. After a short search, we found it, lying in a patch of tall grass. I remember it gazing directly at me as I approached it, and I thought it seemed much calmer than I expected it to be. I got close enough that I knew I couldn't miss, and shot it once more in the head. And that was it. Killing your first moose is very much a coming-of-age event, and my dad was proud. I smiled for pictures, but remember wondering why I didn't feel more excited. I distinctly remember thinking, 'I'm not hungry.' Not just in that moment, but generally: I remember feeling like I didn't *need* to kill it, and something about that unsettled me.

What does it mean to kill a moose when you're not hungry? For years after that, even as I continued to go on hunting trips once or twice a year, I often found myself hoping that we wouldn't see a bull we could legally take. I still enjoyed going out, still enjoyed watching them. I'm not sure if I wished the need to hunt was more definite, or if I wished for a firmer boundary between modern civilization and these wild places.

The local moose seem to be smaller and fewer now, and people don't really catch big king salmon like they used to. Not for lack of trying, either. There are hundreds if not thousands of entrepreneurial guides who will do their best to get one for you, provided you have the funds. A big animal is less often a year's sustenance than an 'experience', a luxurious addition to a life already supported and sustained by other means. Alaska now has international chain stores in most towns, and smooth, fast roads between them; most of its residents no longer live off the land in any meaningful sense. This is a trade-off that has already been made. I have an irrational and selfish wish that no one else should be allowed to move there – that adding more people can only make it worse. This isn't – or shouldn't be – true, in principle, but seems to be in practice. I am not exempt from that. I too drove my gas-powered car, bought whatever I wanted via international traders, paid for university by catching as many fish as possible to be sold thousands of miles away. I am part of the system whose effects I grieve; I participate in it, perpetuate it, benefit from it. And yet I want to create boundaries for it – *go no further than here*. Can't we at least leave *this* bit alone, for ever?

There is still so much space in Alaska – but so little in other parts of the world. People still call Alaska 'the Last Frontier'. If it is among the last unhuman places, surely that is one of its most precious qualities. But the frontier isn't really the frontier any more. Calling it that, treating it that way, feels false. Its wildness doesn't often feel dangerous to me. More often it feels vulnerable, fragile. Something has been lost since the stories I've been told. There are still healthy rivers of fish, bountiful snow, uninterrupted expanses of trees – but nothing has become *more* wild in the last century. Fish populations are partially protected from overfishing, though trophy hunting has had its impact. Forests shrink. 'Natural resources' are weighed against each other by the servants and advocates of The Economy. Places seem always closer to being sold than permanently protected for what they already are. I feel pricked again by hypocrisy as I say that; Alaska and all it holds has been 'for sale' for centuries, under various flags. It's already seen cycles of destructive extraction, from fur-hunting bonanzas to fishing various waters down to nothing, to blasting apart streams and valleys in case rumours of gold were true. I've benefited from those things. I've also done some of the work of trying to put places back together and know how hard it is.

There's a long history of people coming to Alaska to take something and leave. The corporations fighting to open huge swathes of wild land to digging and drilling don't live in Alaska, aren't from Alaska, and won't stay once they have finished. It's a curious kind of entitlement, I think, to believe that the capacity to extract something from the ground means that the ground should belong to you. 'But there's not even anything there,' you'll hear people say; 'It's just miles and miles of empty tundra' – as if the absence of identifiably human projects means there isn't anything to protect or cherish about those places. I've even heard it suggested that mining corporations might simply 'restore' the habitats they ruin, as if it's possible to make something untouched again. As if the difference doesn't matter.

A definitive 'no' does not seem to exist in the public will, so the multinationals press relentlessly on, sometimes faster and sometimes slower, but always knowing it's only a matter of time before their efforts find an amenable political situation. The objections of those whose livelihoods and values would be disrupted are treated as little more than an inconvenience of the trade, to be anticipated and budgeted for. It feels slightly perverse to imagine myself in that position, as one to whom the hopes of a tradition, a way of life, have been communicated, and whose tradition becomes ever more performative and disintegrated as time goes by. I think this is at least partly because Alaska Natives did not have a choice about the changes that were to come, changes that my own ancestors could be considered harbingers in one way or another, fairly or not. But I know my own people loved what it meant for Alaska to be a 'frontier'. They loved that feeling of being out *beyond* civilization, dependent on themselves, their close friends and family, and the land, and in some sense being exposed before God. But that 'frontier life' is largely gone. Perhaps Alaska *was* 'the Last Frontier'. Calling it 'the Last Frontier' suggests that status was always expected to be temporary; that there used to be other frontiers, but those places are no longer what they used to be. They've been taken, changed; their potential both realized and destroyed.

The way of living known by my predecessors, the people who first built houses and farms and lived on those hillside pastures over the bay, is not available to me, not really. The necessity of mutual reliance is gone; the relationship to land always less about dependence, and ever more about its value in trade. Farmland, hunting and fishing grounds alike increasingly become simply real estate as external pressures drive prices steadily up. I am deeply saddened by this. Every additional street light dims the stars, every new building pushes the forest farther away. The world becomes ever more a mirror, the way you can only see yourself in a window when it's dark outside but your lights are still on. I know God remains with me, but I prefer his works to ours.

You can still see wilderness despite the changes. You still see it past the edges of towns, as the houses get farther and farther apart until, finally, you can't see any more of them. You can see it through the changes to the landscape, the buildings popping up, the trees coming down, new roads and parking lots for people to access notable pieces of scenery from their cars. You see the wilderness behind those things, always getting a little smaller. Still vast in many ways, but always receding. I think that might be one of the biggest differences between my generation and those before me; the world already feels quite small to me, finite and precious and much harder to add to than to subtract from. When the sun sets over the Inlet, a shimmering gold-on-pink drips behind always-snowy mountains where, still, no humans have ever lived. And from where you sit on those bluffs, you can't help but feel that you are watching the sun setting past the edge of the world.

11

Endings

AZARIAH FRANCE-WILLIAMS

Close the maternity wards
open up more dementia centres
let us forget
lest we remember
Re-member the passion, the fire, now an ember
the mass movements
obstructing of roads, the power of play
frightening the riot police away
'This is not a riot' one woman stood
to say
It's a funeral, we mourn
no sunshine today
but can we all climb
out of the cold grave
dug by greed's rant
and rave
will humanity rediscover
some vital connection
will we have a resurrection?

PART 2

As It Is Now

12

Soil

EMMA LIETZ BILECKY

Soil joins the future and the past. It is, in the truest sense, the ground of our being and becoming, a community of life making our bodily communities of life go on. Of course, soil is not one thing, but entirely particular in time and in place. Soils exist in infinite compositions of sand, silt and clay particles, elevators of weathering through which underworlds surface. Soils are ever-changing communities of living and dying creatures who leave traces, forge partnerships and respond incessantly to one another in ways that create the environments they share. A healthy teaspoon of soil contains more living beings than there are humans on earth. And just as soil is alive, it shapes our lives – our bodies, economies, politics and cultures – with time. Soil bodies feed human bodies. Soil economies are the genesis of exchange. To the colonizer, soil is territory. To the tongue, soil is *terroir*.

When I was younger, I remember wondering why the places I loved looked the way they did, and how they were different. Why some places – those I thought 'untouched' by humans – felt uniquely sacred, while others – those where I shopped – reproduced in disorienting sameness. Why so much corn grew in the expanse that separated me from my grandparents, and why this deserted sea took ten hours to traverse by car. I never consulted the ground beneath my feet for an explanation. Soil was nothing to me but the setting upon which life played itself out.

Despite our growing intimacy, I am still learning just how much soil is, in fact, life playing itself out – a respiring, decomposing, terraforming force that, though ceaselessly transforming, does not really die. Not only do soil strata, soil bodies and their movements chart layers of deep time, chronicling socio-ecological movements and world-historical events, they respond continually to them – to compaction, excavation, erosion, contamination. Soils are made of memory and of relation. As relational entities, they owe themselves as much to their microscopic members as to their human counterparts. What's more, the land remembers what its human counterparts sometimes conveniently and other times deliberately forget: holding on to our toxic substances and mapping disparities across generations. Whether we acknowledge it or not, we are for ever involved in soil's making and unmaking, as long as we are living, and long after, too.

Soil holds and beholds us, a witness: meeting us, entering us, rearranging our affections, embracing our flesh, crying out. The living encounter the dead en masse here, celebrate at a dirty table. *All this is my body. Take, eat.*

We have invested much in the infrastructures and technologies that allow us to subdue and manipulate soils, enlist them in reproduction to perform reliably and predictably, as a matter of national security, they say. In the USA, this pattern has a long history and a wide reach. From coast to coast, land and soil are reduced to real estate, from the vast, concrete expanse of Los Angeles to the haunted plantations of the South, where long-weathered, clay-rich soils repeatedly farmed to the point of exhaustion trace a westward, deforesting march fuelled by the labour of the enslaved. The ever-intensifying drive towards efficiency, production and specialization strips topsoil from land in ever new and clever ways. Like our bodies, we commodify and sell soil before burying its book-like layers beneath concrete – a kind of sin silencing soil's story with the certainty of the technosphere's perpetual motion. Or, fleeing a lifeless, hegemonic terrain with nothing to hold on to, topsoil runs away through irrupting gullies and mudslides, eroding to meet the rising sea.

This one – I thought dead – is alive. *Were not our hearts burning within us?* This resurrecting body touches me back, unsettling. Still, I doubt, suspended between unknowing and recognition.

In an age called the Anthropocene, I am wooed by oversimplifications, defences against the complexities and complicities asking for my attention. So I measure my life's reverberating impact as a bounded carbon cost, trying very hard to need less, to disturb minimally, to do no harm. By this crude calculus, my body is at best an inconvenience to the 'natural world', at worst sustained by violence against it.

I consider all those my life touches – those who touch me back – the real harm I inflict with my algorithmic movements in an antiseptic world. I look away from these ones I forget in Bad Faith, shunning the living, multiplicitous world *I* (too) *am* for the illusory securities of social distance and internal coherence it shakes. Indeed, there are many who make and maintain me – my ancestors and the microbes, the yeast of the air and protozoa of the earth. We exist together in eternal, self-giving relation, one that ultimately asks everything of me. My grasping, mono-cultural mind resists this yielding. I fear this divine compost.

There is a way that seems right to a person, but its end is the way to death.

Rugged individualism is my sickness, isolating me in time and space and blinding me to the breadth and depth of my relations, to those I owe my being, and those to whom I am responsible in turn. Like others of my generation, I struggle to conceive of the lives of those who would follow me. Becoming mother, ancestor is at times unthinkable. As I anticipate great cost and suffering yet to come, I wish it to stop with me. My life quantified with a dollar sign, I trade comforts for extinctions and ask: is refusing procreation the path to a clear conscience in such a world? Dread and fertility compete for my body as I consider what it means to choose not to go on. But then again, isn't that an impossibility?

Remember: *you are dust, to dust you shall return.*

I am between life and death; both unfold within me. My return to this ground is as quotidian as inevitable. I ease in, bury my pride, behold my loss, and here find I belong to another fertility. Where paths meet and diverge to carve aggregate structure underground, clods of movement and memory coax roots into pattern. Linear lifelines, idols of progress bend to this gravity. There is no end, stop or final solution, only horizons of surfacing memory and ossifying fear. With every breath and every bite we trade carbon for life; with every death we return to the soil.

We are dust and biochar, ongoing disintegration, cycling and for ever entangled. Even so – these threads hurt when pulled.

When they buried our friend in that ground, we all died a little, too. We all die a bit more every day. Let me be always closer to that death, closer to that cold, sun-drenched soil. Let my body, with yours, bear witness, now and then.

13

Farming Grief and Hope

ANDERSON JEREMIAH

Farmer suicide is a burning issue in India, especially among the agriculture and farming community. In the past two decades more than 45,000 farmers have committed suicide, primarily due to crop failures, adverse farming conditions induced by drastic climate change and the corresponding economic impact. Indian farmers depend predominantly on monsoon rains, and if they fail it can have an adverse effect on their livelihood. In many situations, recent studies reveal that failure of monsoon rains is further complicated by rising temperature due to global warming. These adverse climate changes have caused deep anxiety and fear among many farming communities across the country.

Tamil Nadu, my home state in the south of India, is one of the worst affected regions. Having served in several rural parishes in these areas, reflecting theologically on this climate grief was a necessity. Many farmers affected in rural parts of Tamil Nadu belong to Christian communities and often the Church has come up short in providing sufficient support in either understanding their problems or enabling them to address their situation.

My work among some of these communities brought home that the Church in India needs to accept the reality of climate change and recognize how it is affecting its members adversely. Significantly, these communities often tend to be the most marginalized and neglected, the Dalits (formerly untouchables) and Adivasi (indigenous) in the Indian society, so being at the receiving end of climate crisis further undermines their precarious existence.

There are two main theological motifs at play here – solidarity and hope. Reorienting our theological stance from an anthropological to biocentric view would greatly help the Church in equipping rural Christian communities in dealing with climate crisis and address climate grief.

Farmer suicide in India: an overview

Rajkaran Shukla, a 52-year-old farmer from Uttar Pradesh, India, reportedly committed suicide by hanging himself from a tree in his own agricultural field (The Telegraph, 2020). Reports from his family members and villagers provided several insights on the etiology of his suicide. He recently lost two-acre lentil crop out of his four acres land due to water-logging. Similar incidence threatened the remaining two-acre land where he cultivated wheat, necessitating rapid harvesting to save the crop. However, harvesting required laborers who refused to work during the lockdown. Rajkaran was also worried about repaying Rs. 1.5 lacs of debt that he had taken from a private moneylender.[1]

This harrowing account captures the predicament of more than a quarter of a million Indian farmers and agricultural workers who have taken their own lives in the past 15 years. According to the National Crime Records Bureau (NCRB), in 2018 alone more than 10,349 people worked in the agriculture subdivision of unorganized labour in India.[2] In 2018 there were 5,763 farmer/cultivator suicides, about 8 per cent of the total number of suicides across the country. Many of those who died were men and landless labourers in different states, further heaping burdens on women. Significant numbers of these suicides took place in states where the majority of the population depend either directly or indirectly on the farming and agriculture sector. Between 2005 and 2015,

---

1 Hossain, Md Mahbub et al., 2020, 'Suicide of a Farmer amid COVID-19 in India: Perspectives on Social Determinants of Suicidal Behaviour and Prevention Strategies', *SocArXiv*, https://ideas.repec.org/p/osf/socarx/ekam3. html, accessed 11/05/20.

2 See *The Economic Times*, 9 January 2020, at https://economictimes. indiatimes.com/news/politics-and-nation/10349-farmers-committed-suicide-in-2018-ncrb/articleshow/73173375.cms?from=mdr, accessed 08/06/20.

the numbers of deaths by suicide in states central to the agricultural sector were as follows: Maharashtra (17,972), followed by Tamil Nadu (13,896), West Bengal (13,255), Madhya Pradesh (11,775) and Karnataka (11,561). These accounted for 50.9 per cent of the total suicides reported in the country.[3] These states have also experienced significant climate change as much of their agriculture depends on monsoon rains and fields fed by rivers that run dry without much rain. They have also suffered from extreme weather patterns such as cyclones and related flooding, causing significant damage to agricultural fields and livelihoods.

Noted environmentalist Vandna Shiva highlighted the plight of many farmers caused by the violence of the misguided 'green revolution' in the 1970s and 1980s, which industrialized the farming sector by using biotechnology, robbing the natural soil quality and losing significant land water resources.[4] In order to feed the exploding population, Indian politicians forced many farmers to adapt to cultivate cash crops and use intensive mechanized farming. However, these initiatives were all highly subsidized and benefited from cheap labour. Government subsidies began to change with the globalizing neo-liberal free market economy. Smallholding farmers were bought out either by significantly bigger farmers or by landlords with foreign investors to produce exportable food grains. This forced change of pace in farming resulted in unhelpful practices, with extensive use of chemicals and pesticides that had done irreparable damage to the soil. India depends almost entirely upon monsoon rains to feed its rivers, which in turn are the life blood of agriculture and farming in India. Having exploited the ground water resources for intensive farming, the farming community began to depend almost entirely on monsoon rivers. When climate change began to have an impact on regular monsoon rains, rivers started to dry up and land water resources soon became extinct. Water-starved rivers fuelled increased conflicts between different

---

3 G. L. Parvathamma, 2016, 'Farmer Suicide and Response of the Government in India – An Analysis', *Journal of Economics and Finance* (IOSR-JEF) 7(3), Ver. I, May–June, pp. 1–6.

4 Vandana Shiva, 1991, *The Violence of the Green Revolution: Third World Agriculture, Ecology and Politics*, London: Zed Books.

states in sharing water resources. These environmental changes were also fuelled by uncontrolled urban expansion and modern industrial areas being built in erstwhile water reservoirs, affecting traditional irrigation patterns. In all these developments, farmers were affected directly. Wealthy farmers found different ways to survive, but smallholding farmers began to feel the pain. Dwindling governmental aid, lack of agricultural investments, non-availability of other financial recourses, coupled with drastic environmental challenges, have placed a significant burden upon Indian farmers and even pushed them to suicide.[5]

The situation of Dalits and Adivasi farmers is even worse than their counterparts from other communities. The majority of the Dalit and Adivasi community do not have access to land, often ending up in tenant farming, which means they are greatly indebted to the landlord. If their crops fail, they accumulate debt. With repeated failure of monsoon rains, there is little possibility of paying those debts. Many of the farmers from Dalit communities that I encountered during my work in India often end up with huge debts that cannot possibly be repaid. When these economic debts are coupled with climatic changes, it often pushes the farmers over the edge.

Framing farmer suicide as climate grief

Allegedly, after killing his two children, aged 11 and 4, a 38-year-old farmer and his 70-year-old mother committed suicide in front of their house in Kundadam near Dharapuram on the outskirts of the Tirupur. According to police, the farmer, identified as V. Muthusamy, was heavily in debt. For 15 years, Muthusamy had been farming on 2 acres of leased land, police said. In recent years, he had not gotten a good yield and was unable to recover the money he had invested in cultivation. He grew tomatoes and onions depending on the season. He had taken some 9 lakh in loans from various people over the past two years. With interest, he owed 13 lakh, police said.

5 *Times of India* reported that in 2017 alone more than 12,000 farmers across the country took their own lives (3 May 2017).

Unable to make money from agriculture, he stopped farming some months ago and started raising cattle. Meanwhile, his wife Selvi had started working at a textile unit in Tirupur, to make ends meet. 'As he had many loans, money lenders often visited the house. This led to quarrels between Muthusamy and Selvi. A few days ago, after one such quarrel, Selvi left to her mother's house. Frustrated over the matter, Muthusamy killed his two children, Rajalakshmi and Manikasathiyamoorthy, by hanging them from the ceiling of the house, police said. Subsequently, Muthusamy and his mother Myilathal committed suicide outside their house,' police added.[6]

The Indian government frames the issue of farmer suicide as an economic one, citing debt as in the above story. In spite of various studies, the Indian government continues to denounce the link between farmers' suicide and climate distress. Vandana Shiva advocated for adopting a different world view to address the environmental and ecological disaster unfolding in the Indian subcontinent. Shiva argues:

> when the non-sustainability of land use and water use based on extractive logic combines with extreme climate change, we see large scale displacement leading to violent conflicts in our times. The violence to the soil is inseparable from the violence in the society. Living seed and living soils are the foundation of living and lasting societies of sustainability, justice and peace.[7]

I would further this idea to frame farmer suicides not merely as a result of economic issues but also due to climate change. Climate grief is 'the grief felt in relation to experienced or anticipated ecological losses, including the loss of species, ecosystems, and meaningful landscapes due to acute or chronic environmental

---

6 Express News Service, 'Four Members of Tamil Nadu farmer's Family Commit Suicide', *New Indian Express*, 5 August, www.newindianexpress.com/ states/tamil-nadu/2018/aug/05/four-members-of-tamil-nadu-farmers-family-commit-suicide-1853707.html, accessed 26/08/20.

7 Vandana Shiva, 2016, *Earth Democracy: Justice, Sustainability and Peace*, London: Zed Books.

change'.[8] This is very true in the context of Indian farmers. Sadly, the situation following Covid-19 lockdown in India only exacerbated the situation for farmers as more migrant workers have returned to their villages in search of work where many already live a hand-to-mouth existence.

A Christian response: nurturing hope through solidarity

How can we possibly think about nurturing hope in a context of desperation, anxiety and hopelessness experienced by farmers in India? Let me offer some theological insights from an Indian context.

Old cultural sayings often capture and distil a particular culture's world view and moral perspectives. *Nambikkai manithanin thumbikkai* translates as 'Hope is a human being's trunk'. This deeply held view in Tamil Dalit culture captures the belief that hope is central to human flourishing. The versatility and strength of an elephant's trunk suggests that no matter how strong a person is both physically and spiritually, in the absence of hope the person may not have the necessary fortitude to survive. For centuries Tamil culture has valourized individuals who were able to rise above hopeless situations, founded in the confidence that hope is not something external to an individual but found deep within oneself, nurtured by history and tradition. Interestingly, the word *Nambikkai* in Tamil means faith as well as hope. Hope and faith are intertwined. Hope is considered the very ground of existence and being. Hope is the frame of reference through which one makes sense of the world, and hope is not simply wishful thinking. Hope is also characterized by the absence of cynicism. Hope gives life, purpose and meaning. In this regard, hope is a vital life force. Without hope, a person could be considered empty. Tamil epics articulate that hope is

---

8 A. Cunsolo and N. R. Ellis, 2018, 'Ecological Grief as a Mental Health Response to Climate Change-related Loss', *Nature Climate Change* 8, pp. 275–81.

grounded in the community and thrives in relationships, eliminating despair. Hope is essentially communal in nature.

In Dalit communities individuals do not have fenced-off identities but draw their identity from being part of a collective communal identity. In that situation the community nurtures hope. Scarcity of hope generates fear, anger and hatred, which can collapse a community. Breakdown of relationships and fragmentation of communities shatter collective and inclusive identities, opening up space for despair. Despair in turn engenders the human tendency to look inward and develop an exclusive mindset. Hope as described earlier stretches beyond such narrow presumptions and offers the possibility for human beings to reimagine their existence. Hirokazu Miyazaki says, 'Hope suggests a willingness to embrace uncertainty and also serves as a concrete method for keeping knowledge moving in conditions of uncertainty.'[9] Similarly, the Dalit religious world view follows a non-dualist approach to the spirit and human world. Actions in both realms have an impact on all beings. Many Dalit deities were human once and became divine beings through virtues and exemplary lives. The divine beings are not very far away and often involved in human life, thus the prevalence of ancestral worship. This view is not unique to a Dalit religious world view – it is amazing to note that this basic understanding of human existence shapes notions of hope. One could call this view a 'participationist ontology': hope, like all virtues, cannot exist without love and justice. Hope is a kind of love. Just as we cannot privatize love and justice, we cannot privatize hope. Privation of hope is despair. When we despair, our hope becomes deficient and we lose the capacity to seek our objects of hope. Rather, hope should be seen as human moral posturing not wishful thinking. Presumptions are the perversion of hope.

Hope in this context is about pursuit of goodness. Hope is the absence of greed, avarice and pomp, because despair often stems from a lack of acquiring the object of our desire. My Christian understanding of hope was certainly enriched by the earlier mentioned world views, so that when I say from a Chris-

---

9 Hirokazu Miyazaki, 2004, *The Method of Hope: Anthropology, Philosophy, and Fijian Knowledge*, Palo Alto, CA: Stanford University Press.

tian perspective God is central to and the source of hope, I don't simply mean it in a passive receptive manner but in an active pursuit of goodness.

'The God who made the world and everything in it, he who is Lord of heaven and earth, does not live in shrines made by human hands,' Paul declared to the citizens of Athens (Acts 17.24, NRSV). He used a prevalent idea among his audience, by saying, 'In him we live and move and have our being' (Acts 17.28, NRSV), and gave his own interpretation: '[This God] is not far from each one of us' (Acts 17.27, NRSV). Paul captures the very nature of God in these few lines. Gregory Nazianzus said, 'All things dwell in God alone; all things swarm to him in haste. For God is the end of all things.'[10] Christian hope is grounded in this knowledge. The human tendency is to confine, then conquer and control. The divine is not in that desire. The God that Paul proclaimed and encountered in Jesus is not one to be confined or colonized, but right beside us and in the innermost parts of our lives. As much as it is reassuring, the uncomfortable truth is that this God can't be restricted or left behind in the human-made shrines or temples. If we all live and move and have our being in this God, then all of humanity and the universe share in the very being of this generous God. Human dignity and environmental integrity are rooted in recognizing that we have our being in God. To deny this is to deny God's being. This poignant idea is captured in the words of Pope Francis when he addresses our planet as 'Sister Earth' in Laudato Si'. To bring all these strands of thoughts together, the idea of Hope rooted in the community, nurtured through relationships and enveloped and grounded in the being of God, offers the possibility of thinking differently about hope. How can Indian farmers share in this hope?

From climate grief to shared hope

The climate grief of farmers who have taken their own lives in huge numbers signifies falling into the gap of social, political and climate fragmentation. They have lost hope – hope in their lives,

---

10 Gregory Nazianzus, *On the Psalms 3*, in *Patrologia Graeca*, vol. 44.441.

in their communities and in their nation. It is to this desperate situation that hope speaks.

In the Anglican Communion's five marks of mission, the fifth mark says, 'Strive to safeguard the integrity of creation, and sustain and renew the life of the earth.' It is an urgent call for repentance. Churches are called to muster courage to embrace simplicity and sufficiency in our lifestyles as alternatives to the consumerism that is wreaking havoc in our communities, such as farmer suicides. Ecological justice requires us to reimagine our place in the world.

Jesus invites his disciples to express their love by following his commandments (John 17). The God in whom we live and have our being also binds each one of us together in love. The body of Christ is brought to life in the love shared among each one of us; no one is left out, everybody is held together in God's embrace. The best promise from Jesus is that we don't have to do it all by ourselves; we will have the abiding and helping presence of the Spirit of Truth. We need to nurture a culture of hope, where individuals can flourish. Human agency is key to shaping hope. When the Christian world view reorients its theological stance from an anthropological to biocentric view, we recognize that all our future, including the environment, is deeply inter-twined because we dwell and have our being in God. Such a view would greatly help the Church in equipping rural Christian communities to deal with climate crisis and address climate grief.

This chapter began with painful stories of farmers in India pushed to take their own lives due to compounding debt, fail-ure of crops and ultimately environmental change accelerated by global warming. Their situation requires political action to address deeply problematic farming practices based on chemical and industrial fossil fuels, resulting in all sorts of environmental degradation. It needs initiatives keeping desperate farmers and the environment at the heart of decision-making, not industrial-scale farming and profit-driven intensive cash crops. We have no option but to reimagine the relationships between farmers, the community and the environment as one of hope, and so one of justice.

14

Selling Our Souls: How a Scientist Learnt to Lament

TIM MIDDLETON

We used to talk about 'selling our souls'. Someone might ask, for
example, quite politely, over coffee, whether you were tempted
to sell your soul. The answer would be met with a knowing
nod or a wry smile, but no explicit judgement was ever passed.
Looking back, such lurid language seems hardly appropriate for
casual conversation. And yet, when I trained as a geologist, this
was how we all referred to getting a job in the oil industry.

Geology was undoubtedly an exciting subject to study: from
the tectonic forces that sculpted the world's highest mountains
to the exquisite chambers of a fossilized ammonite shell, we
covered a huge range of times and scales. We enjoyed frequent
trips to exotic locations, we listened to some inspiring lecturers,
and there was plenty of engrossing science. We also knew that
oil companies were the principal employers for graduates in our
field: careers events were filled with their representatives; fund-
ing for many departmental activities came from the same place;
and lots of us went on to land good jobs with these companies,
doing interesting work. So why did we all refer to it as 'selling
our souls'?

In Goethe's telling of *Faust*, the devil, Mephistopheles, makes
a bet with God that he can derail the studious Dr Faust. Faust
works hard at the sciences, the humanities and theology, but
he remains frustrated by what he does not know. On returning
home from a walk, Faust agrees to cut a deal with Mephistopheles and signs the contract in blood: Mephistopheles will do

Faust's bidding on earth, if Faust will agree to serve the devil in hell. Faust surrenders his moral integrity, and with it his eternal soul, in return for short-term knowledge and power.

So, is this what my geological classmates and I saw ourselves doing? The short-term pleasures we stood to gain were job security, career progression and a healthy salary. But did we honestly think we were condemning our souls to hell? It all sounds frankly absurd. Perhaps the damnation we were signing up for was knowing that we had contributed first hand to climate breakdown. Indeed, we knew this better than most: one day, we would be taught how to extract natural gas from fractured rock strata; the next, we would be lectured about the devastating impacts that same carbon was having in the atmosphere. The cognitive dissonance was jarring, but talk of soul-selling still feels ridiculous. It was only a job, after all.

And yet, I find myself intrigued by our choice of religious language. With hindsight, it strikes me that there *were* theological elements at play, both in our awareness of climate catastrophe and in our choice of careers – not heaven and hell per se, but a subtler story of deprivation and gain. In brief, what I think our talk of soul-selling reveals is a sense of something lost. And it is this theological undercurrent that I want to explore in the rest of this chapter.

For millennia, theologians and philosophers have had a notoriously hard time defining what they mean by the soul. Is it a rational centre of activity that drives the human machine? A distillation of someone's personality that lives on after death? Or an emergent property of our complex neural networks? As a group of scientific undergraduates engaged in coffee-time conversation we probably didn't have particularly refined ideas of the soul in mind. What we did realize, though, was that *something* was going missing.

We were trained as geologists to envisage climate breakdown in terms of numbers and charts: average sea-surface temperature anomalies and fluctuating isotope ratios in Antarctic ice cores. None of our lecturers got visibly angry, frustrated or upset about the world. The presumption was that detached scientific analysis was the only way forward. Science, we thought, enabled us to understand and manage the planet – but it was no place for showing our emotions.

In the second part of Goethe's *Faust*, Mephistopheles persuades Faust that he wants to control the land and the sea. Faust embarks on a land reclamation project, complete with dams and drainage ditches – and he ultimately succeeds in constructing a castle for the king. Technological know-how, it seems, provides the means for satisfying human appetite. But Faust's desire to retain possession of this reclaimed land – and prevent others from building on it – precipitates a chain of events that eventually results in his downfall and his death. Faust's scientific studies were successful, but they were ultimately insufficient to save him.

So, when we sat in class contemplating climate catastrophe, I think we already knew that science alone was not going to be enough. Many terms of lectures about the climate system had taught us how bad things had got. Whether we were going into the oil industry or not, we could see how hollow our own lives felt in relation to the scale of the problem. No amount of rational thought was going to haul us back from the brink of ecological collapse on its own, and so, in the end, it did not seem to matter what we did with our knowledge and our careers. Our scientific training had not given us the categories with which to respond to this existential news. And this is why, I suggest, we reached for the terminology of the soul. We talked about 'selling our souls' because we sensed that something deeply personal and emotional – some gut reaction inside of ourselves – was already being lost. In short, I think, we were looking for a way to mourn.

For me personally this climate grief manifested itself in several ways. It surfaced as anger and frustration as I tried, with little success, to persuade my department to restructure its careers advice to counteract the influence of the oil industry. It registered as a growing disillusionment with certain scientific mentalities as I first side-stepped into research and then moved on altogether, deciding to pursue a degree in theology. My grief also arose as a kind of denial: a denial of the fact that wherever I was working and whatever I was studying, I was still partaking in a society that was (and is) seemingly incapable of operating without fossil fuels.

The psychotherapist Susie Orbach describes what was going on in this grieving process:

> To come into knowing is to come into sorrow. A sorrow that arrives as a thud, deadening and fearful. Sorrow is hard to bear. With sorrow comes grief and loss. Not easy feelings. Nor is guilt, nor fury, nor despair. Climate sorrow ... opens up into wretched states of mind and heart. We can find it unbearable. Without even meaning to split off our feelings, we do so ... Staying with such feelings can be bruising and can make us feel helpless and despairing.[1]

As scientists, we are especially bad at staying with our feelings because recognizing our own helplessness means relinquishing our sense of control. Like Faust's land reclamation project, we still nurture the hope that science will be sufficient to keep our surroundings in check. Even now, there's still a part of me that is desperate for this to be true. But I have also come to realize that to reconnect with my feelings I must learn how to grieve – to open up to the reality that whatever our species decides to do, there are aspects of our world that are already lost for ever.

This is where the Christian tradition has something to contribute. From the lamentations of the Hebrew Bible to Christ's cry of dereliction from the cross, Christian theology has always been equipped with vocabulary for the articulation of grief. I find the words of the Israelite prophets especially compelling. For example, in Jeremiah's first lament he asks, 'How long will the earth mourn, and the grass of every field wither?' (Jeremiah 12.4, NRSV). Note how agency is given to the earth; it is the earth that is doing the grieving. The Israelite prophets were not conscious of our contemporary climate catastrophe, but what they did recognize were the interrelationships between humanity, God and the earth. The earth is given human characteristics, including the ability to mourn, because it helps us to understand the earth as *related* and *relating*. Treating the earth in this relational

---

1 Susie Orbach, 2019, 'Climate Sorrow', in Extinction Rebellion (ed.), *This Is Not a Drill*, Penguin Books, pp. 66–7.

manner, as if it were another human being, reminds us that we are all part of the same interconnected system. It would never have occurred to a group of geologists to speak in terms of an earth that was weeping or bleeding – science rarely allows for the value of this metaphorical mode of thought – but personification of the planet might just be a mechanism that allows us to *feel* the damage we have done to our home. If what was lacking in our admittedly soulless science was an outlet for our emotions, then the biblical language of earth's grief could have provided us with something to say. Christianity, therefore, not only makes it clear that it is okay to be overcome with sorrow, it also provides us with words that we can use to grieve.

At the end of Goethe's version of *Faust*, the story takes an unexpected turn. Mephistopheles assumes that he has won Faust's soul for eternity, but, at the last minute, angels intervene and take Faust off to heaven. It sounds like a cheap and miraculous interruption, but the angels declare towards the end of the play: 'For he who toils and ever strives/ Him can we aye deliver.'[2] Despite everything he has done wrong, Faust's own striving can still be worthy of redemption. It seems, perhaps, that it is just possible that our souls are not lost after all.

Indeed, the good news is that things are beginning to change. The growing number of professional scientists who are devoting themselves to climate activism goes to show that the need for a more emotional and visceral response to climate catastrophe is gaining traction within the scientific community. Similarly, a project called 'Is this how you feel?' asked climate scientists to hand-write letters explaining how they felt about climate change.[3] Many of these letters still contain facts and figures; plenty of scientists clearly aren't comfortable communicating in an emotional register. As one respondent noted: 'It's probably the first time I have ever been asked to say what I feel, rather than what I think and it's a hard question to answer.' Yet there are also snapshots here of some of the different stages in the grieving process: anger, frustration, despair, exasperation, bewilderment,

---

2 Johann Wolfgang von Goethe, 1839, *Goethe's Faust, Part II*, Leopold John Bernays (trans.), London: Sampson Low, p. 202.

3 www.isthishowyoufeel.com/.

perplexity, fear, vulnerability and tiredness. Intriguingly, perhaps the most commonly reported feeling among this cross-section of climate scientists was hope of some kind. As one scientist put it, it is 'better to light a candle than to curse the darkness'. To me, though, it feels like we need to do both. It is not an either/or decision. We light candles precisely because we have acknowledged and mourned the darkness. Furthermore, cursing the darkness is an important place to start because it indicates a raw honesty about the current state of affairs; realism about the darkness can liberate us to act.

We know that the climate science is well established, and climate chaos has already taken hold. But as scientists, we are only just beginning to learn how to lament. As we struggle to articulate the soullessness of our technical predicament, we are realizing that the climate crisis is as existential as it is scientific. Instead of following Faust and relinquishing our deepest passions to the devil, my proposal is that, as scientists, we should be bringing our feelings and emotions to the table. We may still feel overwhelmed by the scale of the problem but learning to grieve might just be the first step towards regaining our souls.

15

Lament for the Chimanimani Community in Zimbabwe in the Aftermath of Cyclone Idai

SOPHIA CHIRONGOMA

On 15 March 2019, Cyclone Idai thumped on to the Chimanimani Mountains which form the border between Zimbabwe and Mozambique. Torrential rain and sustained winds of up to 190km per hour flattened this low-lying area. It set off landslides that have altered the landscape in the Zimbabwe highlands. Officials in Zimbabwe estimate that 171 people died, 326 have been reported missing, 4,073 people have been displaced and 2,251 houses were destroyed. On 27 April 2019, the Tugwi Mukosi Multi-Disciplinary Research Institute (TMMRI), under the auspices of Midlands State University in Zimbabwe, dispatched a team of 15 scholars to conduct research in order to come up with a true picture of what actually transpired in Chimanimani. As an academic-activist researcher, the following key questions motivated me to join this multidisciplinary research team. How do survivors of the cyclone explain its occurrence and how do they envisage the nature of God? What does Cyclone Idai in Chimanimani teach us about the interface between religion and climate change in Africa?

Although I had been abreast of both print and electronic media reports concerning Cyclone Idai, the magnitude of the disaster hit home the moment we arrived in Chimanimani. We had to use various detours since some of the bridges linking Chimanimani to the rest of the other human communities had been completely destroyed. My heart broke as cyclone survivors showed us where entire sections of settlements had completely disappeared. Massive rocks and stones are now covering the spaces where houses were erected. Images of the biblical flood during the time of Noah raced through my mind as I walked through the valley of dry bones and death in Chimanimani. The overarching question I was left with was: 'How did water, typically understood as the source of life, suddenly become the source of death?'

As described by the survivors of Cyclone Idai in Chimanimani, what started off as an ordinary rainy day suddenly turned into a night of terror, devastation and death. What made the situation worse is that disaster struck between 7 and 8 p.m. in pitch darkness because the heavy rains had disrupted the electric power supply in Chimanimani. Since there was no electric power in the whole town and because the rainy weather had caused an uncomfortably cold breeze, most people had gone to bed early. They were either awakened by alert neighbours or by the mudslides that started flowing underneath the closed doors and filling their houses. Those who survived the catastrophe are the ones who managed to stumble to safety by navigating their way amid the muddy waters in the dark of the night. I listened to horrendous narratives of how families were separated as they helplessly watched some of their loved ones being swept off by the raging waters, mudslides and the gigantic boulders like they had never seen before. I will never forget the stories of how several brave and selfless fellows lost their lives while volunteering to assist children, the elderly and the infirm.

Since the majority of those who survived this calamity in Chimanimani are African Christians, their reflections and lamentations traversed African indigenous world views as well as Christian perspectives on ecological disasters. Some survivors felt the catastrophe had been wrought by the wrath of the ancestors, punishing the people of Chimanimani for wanton destruction of the earth through mining the mineral-rich Chimanimani Mountains. Others surmised that the calamity had been caused by aggrieved ancestors after some local people had desecrated the clay pots that since time immemorial had resided in a sacred cave on Ngangu Mountain, on the outskirts of Chimanimani town. The people of Chimanimani had always enjoyed a cordial relationship with Ngangu Mountain as it was their reliable source of water both for domestic use and for irrigating their gardens and orchards. The boulders and mudslides that spewed from the mountain causing a trail of destruction for the residents of Chimanimani were interpreted as a sign of ancestral rage that needed to be appeased. Such interpretations are informed by the Shona indigenous world view, which understands natural phenomena such as mountains to be the abode of the ancestors: as long as humanity maintains a peaceful and harmonious relationship with the ancestors as well as the earth's resources, they will be guaranteed ancestral protection and sustenance. Conversely, if humanity flouts any ancestral stipulations, especially through either recklessly destroying the earth's resources or worse still desecrating ancestral ornaments, then the ancestors will either withdraw their protection or cause natural calamities. It is against this background that the people of Chimanimani were mourning the broken ties between them and their sacred mountain. They expressed grief because Ngangu Mountain, which had always been their source of sustenance, had suddenly become a weapon of mass destruction.

Several survivors of the deluge interpreted the events wearing Christian lenses. They felt that this catastrophe was God's way of reminding a wayward generation about his sovereign power. Some of them were of the opinion that in the same way God had revealed his sovereignty upon an apostate generation during the time of Noah (Genesis 6.9—9.17), God was reminding the sinful residents of Chimanimani that he still reigns. They concluded that just as some innocent people – especially children – were destroyed for the sins of their generation in the flood during the time of Noah, likewise some innocent folk fell victim to the Cyclone Idai catastrophe.

However, the searing question constantly raised by most of the survivors who lost their homes and their loved ones was, 'Has God reneged on the covenant made with Noah in Genesis 9, when he promised that "I will establish my covenant with you, neither shall all flesh be cut off any more by the waters of a flood; neither shall there any more be a flood to destroy the earth" (Genesis 9.11, KJV)?' In unison with the survivors of Cyclone

Idai and other members of the global community on whose lives has been wreaked havoc by ecological disasters, especially the flood waters, I have continued to grapple with the same question. The scars of an adolescent girl whose rural homestead gave in to the torrential rains continue to be evoked every time I hear about victims of floods. One fateful night, our homestead gave in to heavy downpours. That experience has remained etched in my memory. It had been raining heavily for several days and, as a result, we started noticing some cracks on the walls of our main house whose foundation was probably overwhelmed by the soaked ground. When we went to sleep, nothing prepared us for its eventual collapse in the middle of the night. I remember being awakened from a deep slumber and being informed that our house had just collapsed. Almost everyone in our small rural village promptly gathered around our homestead. In no time, they managed to salvage most of the remaining household items and packed them in a nearby secure house. While my family lost several valuable items when our house collapsed, thankfully no one was injured and no one lost their lives. Although we were fortunate to be enveloped by the support of our neighbours, the trauma of what we experienced as a family on that night has remained very fresh in my mind. I am not in any way claiming to have walked exactly the same path as the survivors of Cyclone Idai. I am profoundly aware that my experience and theirs are different. But it helps me to glimpse the rocky road they have trudged.

Informed by both my Shona world view and my Christian faith, my perspective on the ongoing ecological disasters, especially the floods devastating different parts of the world, is that these are a result of humanity's failure to fulfil our stewardship role. As regards the covenant that God made with Noah during the time of the biblical flood, I believe that God is still keeping his end of the covenant. However, as the old adage goes, 'what goes around, comes around'; as members of the earth community, through the industrialized nature of our economies and the irresponsible extraction of natural resources, we have caused unbearable damage to the ecosystem. In turn, this has come back to haunt us through natural disasters such as floods and earthquakes. I am also reminded of the various Shona taboos and regulations that used to play a fundamental role in preserving the ecosystem. With the coming of modernization, most of these no longer seem relevant, even in the rural communities that are supposed to be the vanguards of indigenous values. Earth's community has now become more susceptible to natural disasters.

Whenever they are confronted with a calamity, it is normal for human beings to grieve over their pain and losses. However, I feel that, as the earth community, our grief over ecological disasters will be futile if we just grieve and fail to engage in deep introspection. I believe that it is time to look at ourselves in the mirror and acknowledge that we have been complicit in causing ecological degradation. In so doing, we will open up pathways for global collaborations of restoration. Our grief should bear fruits of faithfully fulfilling our role as responsible stewards of the environment, and in the process we will restore our relationship with God and with the earth which is God's footstool (Isaiah 66.1).

The survivors of Cyclone Idai, just like many others who have survived from the devastating effects of a world that is dying from the impending ecological crisis, continue to grapple with physical, emotional and spiritual scars. They need words of hope, words of wisdom and, above all, they need helping hands to rebuild their shattered lives. Some elderly parents have been left bereft of economic support after all their children who were working in Chimanimani district died during the cyclone. Several children have been orphaned and some men and women not only lost spouses and offspring but also lost their homes and their sources of livelihood. Their plantations, mining sites, market stalls, vegetable gardens and orchards have all been swept off by the cyclone. Humanitarian agencies, government departments and religious leaders all joined forces to minister to the immediate needs of the Cyclone Idai survivors. However, one year after disaster struck, there is still a yawning gap of material, emotional and spiritual support to the affected communities. Most of them are still battling with the wounds of trauma. These are invisibly deep scars, which call for continual words of life, words of healing and words of counsel.

It is during times of a crisis of such magnitude that faith is shaken to the core. When ministers of religion are serving Cyclone Idai survivors, they ought to exercise utmost caution lest they wound their audience. The Chimanimani community need renewed hope for restoration and rejuvenation. By digging deep into faith reserves, it is my hope that the affected Chimanimani community will be able to find comfort and solace in the prophetic words of the book of Joel: 'I will restore to you the years that the locust hath eaten, the cankerworm, and the caterpiller, and the palmerworm, my great army which I sent among you' (Joel 2.25, KJV).

16

Vida Abundante

PILAR VICENTELO EURIBE

I began feeling closer to creation when I was a child. I lived in emotional abandonment; my parents had too many problems to look me in the eyes and ask me how I felt. I did not feel close to anyone, except for the generous sun, the talkative river and the singer cuculí (bird). God compensated for my loneliness with his glorious creation! I grew up in a town in Peru named Chosica, located close to the capital city, Lima. It has pleasant weather and is usually visited by tourists, but I grew up in a poor house. My father was an alcoholic and my mom did not have a job, so we had big economic problems and domestic violence. It was very stressful for me to see my parents' problems (physical violence) and all I did was to look for places where I could rest my soul. I also felt invisible to them; they were so worried about their own problems that they did not pay attention to me. All of that taught me not to feel like a human, but I could learn otherwise when I connected with the creation. I used to go to the park or take a walk by the river when I was still a child. It was then that I felt the smell of the river and the cool breeze on my face for the first time. I also used to enjoy the sun's warmth among the trees, seeing the blue sky and listening to the singing from the pigeons. I felt alive that way; I felt like a human being and I learned to connect with the creation. This marked my life until I decided to study agronomy when I was 17 years old.

When I studied agronomy I realized I could choose to study agrochemicals that destroy creation, or I could study ways to improve agriculture and respect the environment. I had the opportunity to meet many peasant families in Cajamarca, an Andean region located in northern Peru. I first went to Cajamarca for my pre-professional training with a group of students. I lived in the house of a peasant family for several months. We got up at 4 a.m. to go to the field, and we went to bed at 7 p.m. absolutely exhausted. During the day we used to work the land and we ate in the house, we assisted with their assemblies, we went to their parties, we worked with them and we danced with them. When we had pain, we used to drink a plant for the chakra, and we healed. We sat at the table to eat every night and we warmed our feet by the kitchen fire. We lived among plants and animals and watched the moon, so close to us because we were over 3,500 metres above sea level. They were an example for me because of their hard work and care for the environment, giving me a very special human warmth in return.

> They will build houses and dwell in them; they will plant vine-yards and eat their fruit … my people … will long enjoy the work of their hands. (Isaiah 65.21, 22b, NIV)

I realized that the environment was exploited when I was at university, thanks to my edaphology professor, Juan Zapater. He explained to us that the earth is a living being and that the chemical fertilizers were killing it, destroying the micro-organisms. I was a Christian and I could understand that the earth had been created by God, and human beings were destroy-ing it. Besides, due to my relations with the peasant families, I understood that those actions were going to make them poorer and were going to reduce the crops. I also understood that the agrochemicals destroyed the air, rivers and the health of the farmers and, because they were so expensive, they would make the farmers and peasant families poorer.

For me, climate and environmental pain is indignation in the face of so much indolence; in other words, the bad treatment and the exploitation of the creation, as if it were an object for consumption. We do not value it. We do not appreciate it. We despise it and mistreat it, and it hurts me. It makes me feel indig-nation. I feel that I have to do something and that I cannot stay indifferent. Creation is marvellous; we are part of it, and it needs us. We need it too and we are a unit. Whatever happens to it, happens to all of us and it must be painful for all.

Sin has human, social, ecological and economic consequences, a cosmic and multiplying effect in history and across the planet, affecting the weak, the poor, children and women. Environmentally, this impact is felt with the loss of biological diversity (animals and vegetables), but above all with climate change. There cannot be a separated social restoration or environmental restoration, because they are one unit.

Acknowledging all this, I felt privileged to have the opportunity to help farmers and have the obligation to contribute thinking about other ways to practise agriculture, through a more ecological focus. Then, when I got closer to the word of God and seeing how he promoted rest for the earth, as well as giving us the whole creation for wise administration, I convinced myself that I had to defend creation against so much violence.

> They will not labour in vain, nor will they bear children doomed to misfortune; for they will be a people blessed by the LORD, they and their descendants with them. (Isaiah 65.23, NIV)

My organization, *Vida Abundante*, started back in 2007 when we visited a school in a settlement in Lima's poverty belt. In that school, many of the children were suffering from hepatitis B due to the accumulation of rubbish next to that school. I heard the news on the radio and I went to the school to see what was happening and how I could be of help. As soon as I arrived, I found out that the director was a Christian sister, and we decided to start by making an eco-garden and teaching the children to love their environment, instead of rejecting it. We aimed for a change of attitude and to teach how to relate to the environment, and we did it.

For *Vida Abundante*, we have a vision of 'green' people, producing for their own consumption, where present and future generations have a plentiful supply of resources. This is sustainable development based on a new relationship with the creation. For me, sustainable development starts with a just relation with the environment, which not only brings joy to the soul but also food and knowledge. In Peru, a mega-diverse country, and with high rates of economic poverty, this has huge significance. We must fight to overcome poverty by highlighting the most valuable things of our land. For example, supporting biodiversity through the consumption of ecological products, respecting our seas, and not littering our beaches, taking care of our forest, and defending the vulnerable Amazonian indigenous populations. We need to learn to live in another way, reassuming our relationship with nature from a more respectful and appreciative perspective, living with it, with everything and its creatures. We have to search for abundant life here and now.

17

Grief

DEBO OLUWATUMINU

Her lilting lullabies
cut through
the fog of sleep and apathy,
pierce
the armour of autonomy
that clings to me, a jealous lover,
and summon me.
We are Mayowa – 'The Joy-bringer'
But we have brought Mama
nothing but misery and distress.
Come, she sings,
her once soothing chants
are now a dangerous growl.

The baleful glare of the sun dogged my steps as my feet sank into weary sand. Why here, Mama? Why did you bring me to this soulless, arid wasteland? Precious sweat cascaded down my face. Grains of sand poured down wind-shaped crests and peaks, frozen in time. On the verge of despair, I saw her.

She waited patiently under a stunted baobab tree, shrivelled and dying, skeletal limbs begging an indifferent sky for rain. Mama, mother of creation, sat gracefully on a woven mat of raffia reeds that once grew on a riverbed not far away. Her face, hauntingly beautiful, was a chapped, pitted seabed starved of water. She looked up as I approached, her bright, piercing eyes concealing aeons of unspoken wisdoms, of human seeings and doings, of bloodshed and the unrelenting rape of Cain, filled with tears.

Mayowa …

Her tears, sourced from deep wells of pain and neglect, barely touched her face before they were consumed. Her gaze was kind and motherly. I had heard rumours that she was not well. But nothing like this. True, she had the resilience of the baobab under which she sheltered, but how had such majesty, such splendour, been reduced to this?

I lurched forward, desperate to comfort her, when I saw the baby suckling at her breast. Greedily. Ferociously. I watched, horrified by its monstrous appetite. It suckled without respite and without mercy. In that timeless, sun-baked moment, her breast was both full and withered, as this baby sucked and sucked and was endlessly engorged.

Her face softened slightly at my increasing distress. Sit, her eyes instructed, as she started to sing a Yoruba lullaby that rekindled forgotten memories. But this baby was not lulled. Its will was to consume Mama, wholly and totally, stupidly devouring its way to self-destruction. Loathing rose like lava, intense and piti-less and hateful. I hated this baby. This greedily sucking, selfish, entitled baby. And I pitied her. Mother. I pitied her devotion to life, sworn to cherish and nurture and protect. Without recipro-cation, responsibility or respite? Were we all like this? Mayowa? Are we all like this? Selfish and ungrateful takers?

Her singing stopped abruptly, as if she heard my questions and felt my pity. Her face darkened. She detached the baby from her depleted breast and its angry howl thundered and shook the earth. Tiny fists smashed against her face, her chest, her lips, until it drew blood in tiny rivulets. Stop it! I shouted. Stop it! The baby stopped long enough to spit contempt in my face. A cocoon-like mud basket emerged from the parched and cracked earth and Mama released the still-angry child to its embrace.

Mayowa: Mama, was I like that?

Mama: Every child is different, Mayowa.

Mayowa: But you taught us well! You are not well! Look, Mama! Look! What happened to the rivers, the wildlife, the mighty baobabs? What happened to you, Mama?

She gracefully concealed her pain.

Mama: I sent for you a long time ago, child. Why have you only just come?

Mayowa: We grow up, Mama. We heed our Creator's call to make, to break, to prosper.

Mama: And I have watched your domination over what nurtured you. You are the masters now.

Mayowa: No, Mama, we are mere stewards who forgot our sacred task.

Mama laughed from her belly at my attempts to placate her. I am ashamed. Where did I learn this skill? This ability to overlook the obvious? To repackage misery? To justify selfish desire? Her humourless laughter roused a sandstorm, which carried us south. Swirling crosswinds caught us as we skimmed their silvery backs and dropped us in West Africa, my birthplace; Nigeria, my roots. Mother skipped on to the dead beach as I plunged into a river of sludge. I emerged, spluttering, to find a woman cradling her baby. A fire fuelled by spilled oil cooked contaminated fish on a makeshift grill. The baby stared at me with accusing eyes, as if I were somehow responsible for its noxious meal.

This was once a thriving river. Now dead fish float lazily downstream on its bleached belly. Black sludge bled the river as it expired. Blackened trees claw for breath. Black beaches mourn the loss of grateful dancing feet, communities celebrating fish festivals. I choke on toxic fumes. Grey-black pillars of smoke unfurl. In the distance, a foreign oil well straddles the waters like a giant mosquito, sucking at the heart of the earth.

Mama: Oh, what agony it is for a mother to lose her love for her young, Mayowa.

Mayowa: But we are your children still
We are One with the earth we trample underfoot,
but we are your children still!
To whose embrace do we return
when our living breaths leak
from severed silver cords?
In whose womb were image-bearers
wind-sculpted by the love-infused breath
of Maker, Creator, Triune God?
We are your children still!

Mama shrugs off my heartfelt plea. Her heart has been broken too often. It leaks love now. Her belly rumbles and fire belches from her womb.

Mama: You have learned well how to
plunder tender hearts!
You seductively promise love
but plunder life instead!
Did I not hear the first poisoned whisper
in that virgin sacred space?
When you ruptured a bond of love,
slid across my belly
in search of the cradle of life?
And when you found it,
did you not tear open my bowels
to plunder its precious fruit?
Was I not there when my forests bled
and the heavens screamed
as you tore a hole in my cosmic veil?
Mayowa: Mama, listen –
Mama: No, you have wronged me, Mayowa. The Joy-bringer has brought nothing but death and decay. Why should I nurture and sustain you? Bear your abuse and selfishness? Watch as you plunder and rape without concern? Guardians turned predators? Why should I not deplete your rivers and streams? Sterilize fish eggs and desiccate tree seedlings? Why should I purify the air you breathe while you smother me?!

The skies grew black with Mama's ancient pain. What could I say to relieve this roiling grief? To whom will I appeal? Bleached skulls, congealed streams and slaughtered trees? This ravaged jury awaiting righteous judgement? Contrition is my humble offering. We are guilty.

Mayowa: You are right to be angry, Mama. But remember, our people say, even the mother of an errant child cannot deny her young. You must forgive us. We know now the cost of fatal curiosity.

Mama: You have come too late to a quarrel lost.
Faithless Man has squandered nature's trust,
so now I turn deaf ears!

Where were you when I groaned
under Cain's relentless blows, Mayowa?
My Creator's excited
Good! Good! Good!
is lost in the shadows of time!
Where were you when I howled
under Cain's vicious strikes?
Is there not enough for all?

Thunder rumbled as she bellowed, daring a response, an excuse, a defence.

Mama: These babes! These gullible slaves to thirsts and hungers that drive their lusts! See their scoured scars across my back? The back that rocked them to sleep? That protected them, these ungrateful tyrants of the universe? These bottomless bellies? These – !

Mama! My heartbroken cry silenced the thunder and momentarily slaked the brewing storm. I watched her reach for the blackened fish smouldering on the fire and feed fish pulp to the silent child. And I wept, the baby's eyes fixed on me. Can we learn this lesson? Turn back the implacable hands of time? Three crosses impale the ancient hill of skulls. It. Is. Finished.

Mayowa: Listen, Mama! Can you not hear his cry on that ancient hill of skulls? Did you not receive his dreaded drops of blood? Were you not moved by his cosmic pleas of peace?

Mama: Stop –

Mayowa: Guilty, Mama! We are guilty!

Mama: Yes! Yes, you are!

Mayowa: But true Adam embraced creation's pain. Death choked on Love's life! The poisoned whisper now invites creation's praise!

Mama: But you don't listen! Did I not teach you well? Raise you well? You're bloated with pride, Cain's blind brood!

Mayowa: But love enlightens our darkened eyes, Mama! We see better now! Divine blood flows freely through mortal veins. Forgive us, Mama –

Mama's face contorted. In her eyes only despair, disbelief, distrust – and, and – and I was done. Her scarred back is turned to me. The grey-black clouds are darker still. I am spent. Perhaps love has its limits after all. Perhaps we have crossed the horizon and fallen off its edge. But still I try.

Mayowa: Please, Mama. We will do better, for God's sake, who works and so we work, to put his world to rights.

Lightning crackles over clouds of methane and I turn away.

Mama: Mayowa.

I turn back wearily as Mama slowly turns to me, a flicker of hope rekindling in her ageless eyes. What mother denies an errant child?

Mayowa, Children of the Earth – Listen! Inaugurate the ancient Jubilee! Creation waits with bated breath for the unveiling of the love-bought children of God. Mama's tears are a cleansing rain. A new morning dawns: a boat sits at sea and a man cooks fish ashore. A servant king, inviting us to straddle heaven and earth to soothe creation's grief. Roll up your sleeves then, Mayowa, Joy-bringers, and get to work!

18

Water of Life in South Korea

SEOYOUNG KIM

South Korea has experienced ongoing local climate change and extremes in weather variations. The annual temperature is increasing, and the summer is becoming longer: we suffer from extremely hot temperatures, drought and unpredictable precipitation such as flooding and typhoons. In particular, farmers like my grandfather are affected by severe water shortages, caused by drought, and flooding and typhoons, which destroy crops and contribute to environmental damage. He has engaged in rice farming since the 1950s, but he is getting more worried about his work, particularly crop-yield reduction, due to drought and the uncertain weather. He frequently tells our family that 'it is tough to anticipate weather these days, unlike the past'. Like other farmers in South Korea, he lives with climate anxiety, despite not contributing to the industrial and developmental culture that has damaged our environmental harmony and led to climate change.

Climate change is not only affecting people: fishes, birds, and all kinds of living beings are even dying of thirst in the intense heat, and many have left their usual habitats. The biggest reservoir in South Korea, Yedang Reservoir, dried up 92 per cent of water reserve rates during the drought in 2017. Many fish died.[1] Climate anxiety – fear for survival – is spreading to all life on earth: water unites all living beings and all places, and the threat of death due to lack of water exposes how dependent we are. It

---

[1] Sunjae Kwon, 2018, '"Preparing for the Drought" Chungcheong Province Works for Agricultural Water Supply Project', *Kyunghyang News*, 18 November, https://news.khan.co.kr/kh_news/khan_art_view.html?artid=201811181 133011&code=620112, accessed 17/07/20.

is impossible for us to live without water for more than about 72 hours, and yet we fail to protect it.

As water scarcity increases, those suffering from poverty and other structural oppressions are most affected. Water becomes a resource for luxury and used to increase the ease of the privileged minority, indifferent to the anxiety of the majority underprivileged. If we are to ease the suffering of the most vulnerable creatures, a hydro-centric perspective of creation will teach us to better understand the ethereal web of life.

The challenge of a hydro-centric perspective is not just a way of managing resources better, but a therapeutic call to read the Bible in a new way. The story of creation describes water as already existing before the earth (Genesis 1.2). The water of life is dynamic, not static; it is continuously moving between the atmosphere, land and sea (Genesis 1.6–8). The cycle of water sustains the life of all creation. In the book of Psalms, it is written that water resources, springs and the sea are part of the cosmic liturgy of praise (Psalm 148). The book of Exodus tells us that water is also redeemed by God, who made water drinkable at Mara (Exodus 15.22–27). Jesus, God incarnate, is blessed by water at his baptism (Mark 1.9–11). He describes himself as living water, a giver and source of eternal life (John 7.37–38). The whole of creation longs for this water of life, which flows freely in the river of the promised new Jerusalem (Revelation 22.1–2). Focusing on water in order to develop a hydro-centric theology is not intended to be reductionist, or replace anthropocentrism. Instead, a hydro-centric hermeneutic helps us to develop responses to the grief of the thirsty earth, bringing healing for climate anxiety and refreshing the Church's dimensions of mission.

This hydro-centrism will need to be an antidote to the social and theological issue of indifference. Sadly, most people in South Korea do not take climate change issues seriously. They are only frightened when they face unpredictable environmental problems, but they do not attempt to tackle the fundamental causes of climate change. Organizations such as the Korean government, companies, social groups and the National Council of Churches in Korea say they are concerned about climate change issues. Yet, only a few individual people and local churches sincerely respond. Most still treat climate change as a problem for the future. In order to respond to gradual climate change, we must repent of our human-centred lifestyles and abandon the pursuit of excessive economic growth. By learning from and protecting water, a free gift which sustains us all, we might learn to change.

As a Presbyterian, I long to see Korean Protestant churches seeking climate justice together and thereby bring social healing for climate anxiety. The Korean Protestant Church has divided into around 370 denominations, most of which pursue narrow individualistic salvation while choosing to ignore the universal and cosmic dimensions of salvation. They are focused on themselves and the afterlife, rather than seeking healing for all creatures and this world. This other-world-centred and self-centred faith leads Christians to disregard climate change and refuse to acknowledge the earth's grief. However, we are called to be water of life, meeting both physical thirst and spiritual thirst.

As we seek living water, I want to offer a prayer for the Korean Church, that we might learn to grieve, repent and seek peace for all creation.

Prayer

Lord,

The earth was formless and empty, darkness was over the surface of the deep, and the Spirit of God was hovering over the waters.[2]

Thank you for creating the earth, and the atmosphere, the sun, moon and stars.

Let there be a vault between the waters to separate water from water.[3]

Plants, birds, animals and humans; we all belong to you.

---

2 Genesis 1.2 (NIV).
3 Genesis 1.6 (NIV).

Let the water teem with living creatures, and let birds fly above the earth across the vault of the sky.[4]

Let the land produce living creatures according to their kinds: the livestock, the creatures that move along the ground, and the wild animals, each according to its kind.[5]

Highest heavens,
and the water
above the highest heavens,
    come and offer praise.[6]

Forgive us, O Lord.
We are destroying the earth.
We pollute the sky with aeroplanes and the earth with vehicles.
We build buildings and factories.
We cut down trees.
We hunt birds.
We kill animals.
We are not loving our neighbours.
We are not listening to the groans of your creation.

Moses led Israel from the Red Sea and they went into the Desert of Shur. For three days they travelled in the desert without finding water. When they came to Marah, they could not drink its water because it was bitter.[7]

Have mercy on us, O Lord.
We are suffering from global warming.
We face unpredictable seasons, extreme weather and natural
    disasters.
We are thirsty.
We are dried up.
All your creation is dying.

---

4 Genesis 1.20 (NIV).
5 Genesis 1.24 (NIV).
6 Psalm 148.4 (CEV).
7 Exodus 15.22–23 (NIV).

Then Moses cried out to the LORD, and the LORD showed
him a piece of wood. He threw it into the water, and the water
became fit to drink.[8]

Convict us, O Lord.
We do not want to sin any more.
We do not want to dominate the earth any more.
We do not want to seek other gods, such as wealth and power,
    any more.
We do not want to be indifferent to your creation any more.

Jesus said, *'Let anyone who is thirsty come to me, and let the*
one who believes in me drink ... "Out of the believer's heart
shall flow rivers of living water".'[9]

Help us, O Lord.
Please guide us and give us wisdom and courage.
Teach us how to live together in peace, and in harmony with all
    your creation.
In Jesus' name, Amen.

The river of the water of life, bright as crystal, flows from the
throne of God and of the Lamb through the middle of the street
of the city.

On either side of the river is the tree of life.

And the leaves of the tree are for the healing of the nations.[10]

---

8 Exodus 15.25 (NIV).
9 John 7.37–38 (NRSV)
10 Revelation 22.1–2, adapted from the ESV Bible.

19

Tears of the Natives: (Is)lands and (Be)longings

JIONE HAVEA

Covid-19 is the latest crisis to reach Pasifika (Pacific Islands, Oceania). In the early days of the Covid-19 pandemic, as we were learning to understand the demands of the 'new normal' – driven by fear and amplified by economic downturns, social distancing and border closure – Cyclone Harold upturned the lands and seas of the Solomon Islands, Vanuatu, Fiji and Tonga (2–9 April 2020). The cyclone (categories 4 and 5 over different waters) did not mind that a new virus was 'in the air', carried across borders by travellers and migrants, nor did it respect the sovereignty of islands and their borders. A harsh reminder of the ecological crises that trouble all islands in the region, and beyond, before and in the midst of the Covid-19 pandemic.

Once Harold passed and locals began to pick up the pieces and grieve over the destruction to our sea and island homes, one of the concerns that circulated was how Covid-19 has distracted (or has been used as a scapegoat to distract) the world from the crises of global warming. It is especially painful for Pasifika natives that before 31 December 2019, when the new corona-virus was reported to the WHO, major world powers were stingy and hesitant to join the movements to reduce toxic pollutions and clean up the air, the land and the waters; but as soon as Covid-19 is seen as a threat to human profits and investments, these world powers pump out rescue packages in the millions. In my native brown eyes, this says that humans are worthy of rescue but the world in which we live does not deserve a collaborative global effort to clean it up. That does not add up: how effective are attempts to rescue the human species without also caring for (maintaining, sustaining) the habitats that humans share with many, many other species?

I do not deny the havoc and pain that Covid-19 is causing, but i also take the pandemic as a new space for reflection.[1] My attention is directed to the 'tears of the natives' and i use 'tears' in two ways: as evidence of crying and as the result of shredding. In the following sections, i explore three clusters of *tears* – designation and label, myths and location, home and identity.

Tears in banners

'What's in a name?' does not feel appropriate to many Pasifika natives. In Pasifika, native names are reminders of the ancestors and their journeys. Names are passed on to coming generations, and some names are changed when situations make old names irrelevant or shameful. Similarly, new names come up in response to life situations. For Pasifika natives, there is a lot in each name, whether the name is given to a body, a place, a home, a collaboration, a phenomenon or a crisis. Names are more than just labels.

With regard to the ecological crisis at hand, naming it 'climate change' or 'global warming' makes a difference in native ears. It is 'normal' that the climate *changes* over the seasons of the year (associated with tasks like planting, harvesting and fishing), and it is also expected that the weather turns in each season (for example, it might rain during the dry season). To borrow the native wisdom of Qoheleth, there is a time for everything under the sun (see Ecclesiastes 3.1–8). Changes are normal, so why should anyone make a fuss about 'climate change'? Put this way, it is easier for some folks to deny the current ecological crisis or to take it lightly. Those deniers do not see the burden that smaller nations – especially in the Global South, where their contribution to pollution is disproportionate to the devastation that

---

1 I use the lowercase for the first person when 'i' am the subject, in the same way that i use the lowercase for you, she, he, it, they and other. Contrary to English grammar, which is foreign to Pasifika, i cannot find justification for 'shouting' (with a capital letter) the first person subject.

they face – bear for the global community. The question from natives is clear: why should we suffer for the sins of the world?

The label 'global warming' reminds the global community that the ecological crisis is a shared burden. The signs are everywhere – from droughts and famines to extra heavy monsoons and more frequent and more powerful storms pounding shores everywhere (Cyclone Amphan, which tore into West Bengal, India and Bangladesh on 19–20 May is the strongest storm to hit the region in more than a decade). The 300+ children who die *each hour* (according to WHO) due to malnutrition (as the result of famines, unfair production and distribution) include many children (mostly black and ethnic minorities) in the shadows of modern empires; soil erosion displaces communities along the Nile and the Ganges as well as along other rivers and valleys; sea levels rise on the shores of islands as well as on the shores of continents; fires are killing millions of animals and plants in bushes and forests all over the world; etcetera, etcetera. The struggles that global warming brings are as troublesome to the peoples of Mombasa, Mumbai and Manilla as to the peoples of Miami, Medellín and Milan. Global warming *is* a global crisis, and in my native brown eyes no virtual bullying or fake news can deny or shift the blame.

The preference for the global warming label does not negate movements under the climate banner (climate justice, climate refugees, climate trauma, climate grief, and so on). The push for climate justice should not be drowned in the waves of some configuration of global justice according to which justice is defined to serve the interests of the powerful; and the legal status and rights of climate refugees needs to be recognized alongside political refugees in and by international law. Global warming is more than mere rhetoric; global warming is more than a topic or an issue; global warming is a matter of life and death. When anything distracts from this crisis, it tears up the hearts of natives.

Tears from diaspora

'Our ancestors were navigators' is one of the proud affirmations that modern Pasifika natives make. We have legends and so-called tribal artworks that tell of their skills and courage, and each island group has their own versions. It is not required of legends to be in unison in order to be meaningful. One of Pasifika's beloved ancestors is Maui, the demigod who fished the islands up from the *moana* (deep sea), who brought fire up from the womb of the land and who pushed the sky upwards so that life unfolded on earth. Before Disney made a big profit from selected versions of the legends of Maui in its 2016 animation *Moana*, Maui was remembered in the name of islands, people and corporations as well as in tattoo patterns and other forms of art. One of the characteristics shared by the legends of Maui is that he was a navigator who crossed the seas.

Affirming that Maui and our ancestors were navigators is one way of saying that they came from somewhere else. Legends name their places of origin (Hawaiki, Avaiki, Havai'i, Pulotu, Burotu) but no one knows where those are located. They are legendary, mythological, places; those are places to which they (be)long rather than places from which they originate. Our legends are myths of belonging rather than myths of origin; our people are not (ab)original to the islands where we have grown up. For our navigating ancestors, Pasifika was the diaspora; and we have become natives of discovered (is)lands. In my case, i am a native Tongan, but my navigating ancestors came from some-where else. Our people are not indigenous or aboriginal (hence my preference for 'native') to Tonga; Tonga is our home, but not our possession. Tonga was the diaspora for our navigating ancestors. This applies to all other native islanders who share the legends and pride that our ancestors were navigators.

Fast-forward to the current ecological crisis: one of the cries that comes out of the most vulnerable island groups, like Kiribati and Tuvalu, is: 'What are we to call ourselves after our island homes drown in the waves?' What will it mean to be called Tuvaluans when there is no longer an island group named Tuvalu? This question is about identity. The same question applies to the natives of Kiribati (as a group), as well as to the natives of villages and smaller islands (within island nation states) that have been, or are expected to be, resettled because of uninhabitable conditions brought about by global warming. Who are they after their island home has disappeared? While i am in deep solidarity with displaced natives, this reflection asks a critical question of native people as well: is the pain of climate grief evidence that natives have forgotten what it meant for our ancestors to live in diaspora?

Tears for tomorrow

In reggae speak, 'Tomorrow People' is one of the designations for the future generations. Ziggy Marley titles one of his works 'Tomorrow People' and asks two questions in the chorus: 'Tomorrow people, where is your past?' He then asks them how long they will last. These are important questions: to know the future requires that one knows the past first.

The cry of the natives is intensified by not knowing our past. The cry is painful because native customs and identity intertwine with the island home, and the loss of (is)land is more than just a matter of losing ground.[2] Loss of (is)land is also about the loss of the foundations and frames for meaning and belonging. Loss of (is)land involves the loss of (be)longing.

In this age of migration, the sons and daughters of Pasifika live and die scattered across the world. Those natives (in the modern-day diaspora) are Pasifika's Tomorrow People, and they are already present. Their question is slightly different: 'Where is home?' Their question is about belonging. This question is *tear*ing because, for some of them, the home island of their (grand)parents no longer recognizes them (that is, out of sight, out of mind) and, also, their adopted homeland does not fully embrace them and their differences (the lot of migrants). And with global warming gnawing at the home island as well as at the

2 I expand on this concept in *Losing Ground: Ruth in a Changing Climate* (London: SCM Press, forthcoming), a collection of Bible studies that draws upon native insights into the challenges of global warming.

adopted homeland, their grief will suffocate them. The future for Pasifika's Tomorrow People is grim.

So what?

The future may be grim, and distractions will continue to rise on the horizons, but it is not in the nature of natives to give up. Natives giving up is an illusion of colonialists. Natives survive catastrophes, including the whitewash of colonialists and missionaries, and global warming and Covid-19 are the current tests of our time.

I do not refer to these crises as 'signs of the time', because that biblical expression carries apocalyptic end-time connotations. Whether in the mouth of Jesus (Mark 13.32; Matthew 24.7; Matthew 24.24; Luke 21.25–26) or of a disciple (2 Timothy 3.1–4), this biblical expression refers to a great tribulation at the end of time, at the end of the world. These crises – global warming, Covid-19 and Black Lives Matter – are devastating, and they will linger for some time, but i am not prepared to say that they mark the end of time. They are crises in our present contexts, and this reflection invites that we take them into account in our theological and pastoral work. As humans, it is expected that we see things in and work for our own interests. But that is not justification for tearing earth up.[3]

Global warming will pick up speed again once the Covid-19 pandemic settles down and the machineries of our carbon civilization are switched back to full speed. To stop the *tear*ing of the world, global collaboration is required. Tears will multiply, but tears do not have to have the final word. Nor the final world.

---

3 See Brooke Fryer, 2020, 'As Protests Raged across the US, Donald Trump Quietly Wound back Environmental Protections', SBS *News*, 11 June; www.sbs.com.au/news/as-protests-raged-across-the-us-donald-trump-quietly-wound-back-environmental-protections?, accessed 14/06/20.

20

The Hills are Alight

DIANNE RAYSON

I wake up and can't see the sunrise for the smoke. The mountain is on fire but it's still winter. I head down to the creek bed that is dry, dry. Bone dry and littered with bones. Scapegoats on the altar of coal. I take off my shoes and my feet hold the smooth river rocks, suffocating in the air. I am on holy ground.

Solastalgia describes the homesickness for place that you experience while you're still at home. Where nostalgia is a reminiscence for home when one is far away, solastalgia is entirely in place: but the place is hardly recognizable. Glenn Albrecht coined this word to account for the grief and distress of the folk in the Upper Hunter – my birthplace – as the open-cut coal mines destroy the unique black soil farmlands and horse studs. Where communities are bulldozed and where so-called restoration of old mines leaves dead trees stuck in refilled pits of clay. The earth burns there: the coal dust is alight underground and nothing will ever grow in that wasteland.

My place has changed too, is changing, and the grief I feel is the sadness for what was and is no longer. I am losing my home. We all are.

In the middle of the year, while it was still cold in the southern hemisphere, the mountains behind my farm caught alight. Years of drought had sucked the water out of the forests. As the Indian Ocean heats and the Dipole increases, the rain ceases to fall across our dry continent. The kangaroos had already moved in, down to our farm and others, sourcing the water that remained in our dams (ah, there was still water in the dams then). Some twilights would have them visit the house, nibbling what remained of my forgotten flower beds. Little joeys popped out of mummas' pouches, not knowing what was ahead. None of us did.

The fire started in a tiny location in the forest, probably from a lightning strike in these storms that now typify our life. Dry storms with lightning. They warned us of this. They warned us of it all. Week after week, our little fire moved across the mountains, through the state forests, through national parks, along creek valleys.

That's when the smoke started. Months ago. By the end of spring, the fire, now named Rumba Dump, bore down on the village communities that populate what was once rich dairy country. The dairy farms are mostly gone now – first going broke from a dysfunctional dairy industry that favoured international consortium megafarms, and finally from drought. Farmers moved to the small herds of beef cattle. Some are chicken farms, some a few mixed animals and crops. Some, like us, just like having cattle around to eat the grass and care for their young. Grass. It was waist deep those summers and so green it hurt. Not now. The paddocks are crunchy and grey, the soil as powdery as flour as it blows away. Old farmers look the same. Grey and crackly. Dreams long blown away and only persevering because farmers always have. But not all of them. We lose them too, more victims of the drought. More dry bones.

We all grieve and we're all homesick for our land, our country. Well, not really *our* country. This is Biripi land, stolen two centuries before. Those bones again. Even the stories are stolen. I can't tell you the names of those who walked and loved this land before me and I don't know their stories. I can't see the subtropical rainforest for it is long gone too, harvested for timber and replaced with paddocks. Along with the ancestors, we're all solastalgic here. The land is parched and the mountains on fire; our way of life, precarious.

The wind churned the sky to a dark, greasy orange grey and we couldn't breathe, but we stayed outside to watch for embers. The leaves flying around us were black and bubbled and foreigners. Leaves from Rumba Dump, messengers of what was coming.

The power fails, of course. Falling limbs. Neighbours share small generators and check on each other. We move our extra water pump and hose into place (the firefighter we call it), on a trailer attached to the quad bike. Fire hoses rolled out, systems tested. No internet, no phones, no news. Just an atmosphere of grime and harm and dread.

And so we didn't know that in the very next valley homes were being lost, one after another. The old school where Uncle Ray had been the single teacher mid-century – gone. People escaping through flames, hiding in waterholes, houses alight. We could see the great plumes of smoke but couldn't know that cattle were dying, chickens, goats, cats, dogs. Koalas and possums, echidnas and platypus, all victims. Birds and flying foxes falling from the sky. Snakes and lizards came nearer the house for water. Folk needed shelter and came across to our valley: a car packed with cats in boxes; a motorbike with nothing else; a hermit from a cave up on the mountainside who lost everything but his humour. We housed the refugees and the next morning set out to share the little hay we had with the cattle stranded on black earth, hoof deep in ash. Fences burned to the ground but where were the cattle to go? Escape to what? Water tanks melted like giant grotesque accordions; what was once a home with pot plants and prized show chickens, pet cockatoos and an outdoor swing for the grandchildren, now a nightmare of mangled grey metal with the odd shard of crockery or a headless garden gnome. We woke in the overalls we slept in, boots on our feet, bandana over our faces. We slept in shifts, one of us walking the vicinity of the house and sheds. The sky was starless to us. As the clock ticked over one night and it was past midnight, it was my birthday. I wondered if I would live through the day. I checked the pumps, checked the size and position of the flames, checked on my dog.

From his tiny prison cell in Germany in World War Two, Dietrich Bonhoeffer smuggled out theological letters that explored what Christianity might look like after the Holocaust. Worldly Christianity, he called it. A faith that sets aside the failings of religion and its institutions and instead lives a fully engaged life in this very world. Living before God but *as if there is no God*, he said. Learning to speak about Christ in a new way, where religion is no longer the default position but instead sees Christ in the face of the other. Living a responsible life that takes seriously the ethical imperative of being-for-others.

Standing on my land at night, in this smoke, I wonder how Bonhoeffer would think about climate change, had he not been martyred, and my drying, burning country. The new language of ecology reminds me of the old language of Trinity and interrelationships, holiness and sacredness of earth and land. The continuity of indigenous spirituality that recognizes the Great Spirit in and through all of creation and the old hymn in Colossians: in Christ all things were created and all things hold together; through Christ all things are reconciled to God. A worldly Christianity in the Anthropocene becomes an earthly Christianity that speaks the language of Christ in and through earth, just as our ancestors perceived and our scientists describe. An earthly Christianity that speaks into the relationships we have with our land, the animals we share it with, the plants and birds and the fungi under our feet who share their stories with the trees. A new way of speaking of Christ as the author of the Dark Emu in the Milky Way and whose stardust builds all life on earth.

Earthly Christianity takes the grief of solastalgia and lets it be, recognizing that violence and greed have painful consequences. The inevitability of death is what makes us love life just as grief highlights love: *tob and ra*. 'Even tears of bliss are salty', Bonhoeffer says. But earthly Christianity won't stop there. It's a faith that continues to hope in a resurrection and works for a kingdom of God to blossom into life. It's a faith that restores relationships with land and animals and communities, and partners with Christ in such reconciliation. Now we understand the whole biosphere as interconnected. There can be no others now, we are all one body.

It's Christmas and we can't drive to the nation's capital because the highway is closed: more bushfires. Homes destroyed, lives lost, volunteer firefighters exhausted, and still the government shows no compassion and simply won't act. How can this even be? Ah, but there's a direct connection to our original sin in this country: our euphemistic dispossession of an ancient people who walked and sang this land for tens of thousands of years.

Possession doesn't describe relationships or the spiritual connection between people and country. In our conquest and slaughter of indigenous people, we thought we could master nature as well; we were fools.

I get up early, pump the last of the brown littered water into a tank for the cows since the creek is dry, dry. They lick my hands as I hand feed them hay and molasses and they know it's Christmas. I wonder if they feel the solastalgia too. On the hills, new plumes of smoke rise to the sky.

Postscript

The summer of 2019–20 became Australia's Black Summer. The east coast was ablaze, and other states too, until mid-February when the rain finally came. Hundreds of thousands of square kilometres were alight and images of tornadoes of flames and great walls of fire touched the hearts of many around the world. Nearly 3,000 homes were razed and 34 people lost their lives; whole communities stranded on beaches and day turned first to blood-red then black of night as smoke choked the sky. A billion animals succumbed: species already on the brink may have been pushed into extinction. Whole forests have been lost for ever: there is not always recovery.

Our own fires were seemingly forgotten as records broke: hottest days, hottest nights, worst air pollution in the world, worst fires in our history. We thought Black Summer would be the turning point in our fight against coal, against rampant capitalism and pollution, against hubris and vested interests, but we were wrong. The politicians and the media soon moved on. The world has warmed by one degree, but even more on this continent, and seasons like this are our inevitable future. Australia has become the canary in the coal mine.

21

Climate Grief – Climate Guilt

HUGH JONES

In early December 2013, my family and I were living in Boston in south-east Lincolnshire. This part of the world has always been vulnerable to flooding. Geographically, it is the northernmost part of a swathe of low-lying marshland called the Fens, land drained by humans to transform it into farmland that produces a significant proportion of the UK's food. This essentially man-made landscape has an austere beauty, its vast skies and long sight lines punctuated only by water towers and farm machinery. It is a far cry from the stereotypical image of rural England.

Keeping water off the soil has been a way of life here for centuries, but the job is getting harder. Recent forecasts suggest that much, or all, of it could disappear if global temperatures continue to rise. Sea levels are certainly rising, and anecdotally at least there is a sense that dramatic weather events are becoming more commonplace in this part of the world. We lived through one of those events that December.

Our home was on a street near the Haven, the tidal estuary of the river Witham, a few miles from the North Sea. On the far side of the Haven stood St Botolph's Church, known as 'Boston Stump' and one of the miracles of late medieval English archi-tecture. Our back garden was several feet below the top of the riverbank on the far side of the fence. As we looked out of our back windows at high tide, the water level was well above our ground floor. Our home and the church in which I'd served as curate for three and a half years were both within a few yards of flood defences that were visibly threatened by the highest tides.

During the course of the day on Thursday 5 December we received calls from the Environment Agency both on the telephone and in person, advising us to take action to protect our belongings and to evacuate if possible. It was already raining hard, and the rain combined with the anticipated 'tidal surge' had led to a severe flood warning being put in place.

We moved most of our possessions upstairs as quickly as possible, but by the time we left to go to stay with friends, water was beginning to pour over the flood defences. Within a few hours, our street was a fast-moving river. By the morning, the famous Stump tower was standing in a metre of water. We returned home to discover that the house had escaped serious damage, but the opposite was true of the church. As the waters gradually subsided, the clear-up began, and with it the recriminations.

Some blamed the Environment Agency, others attributed everything to climate change, while others found smaller details to criticize. This need to find fault was among the first reactions to the catastrophe. I recognized it as a symptom of grief, a response to physical and emotional loss that bore a clear family resemblance to bereavement. The reactions to the local environmental catastrophe of Boston's flooding, and the wider disaster of climate change, represent a form of bereavement in which guilt and blame play an important part. I have two particular suggestions to make about this. The first is that acknowledging and handling this aspect of the grieving process well is an essential part of being able to adjust positively to the world after loss. The second is that the Christian tradition offers rich resources to that end. Indeed, as a Christian priest, I believe it provides the only fully satisfactory way of doing so.

In my work as a parish priest, I encounter grief on a regular basis. As someone whose background is in psychology, I also know that grief is not one emotion but many, having elements of anger as well as sadness, of guilt as well as gratitude. While Elisabeth Kübler Ross's 'five stages of grief' may not be a strictly sequential experience in every instance, her identification of the different elements of the grieving process remains helpful when providing pastoral care to the bereaved. Climate grief is no exception. Denial is in abundant evidence. When grieving, people refuse to accept that what is happening to them is real. Denial provides them with a layer of emotional protection. Anger is also plain to see. When grieving, people who have understood that their loss is real look for someone to blame, someone to punish for what has happened to them. Anger provides us with something to do.

The aspect of grief that I find most interesting, however, is guilt. Of all losses, the loss of opportunity for reconciliation is often the hardest to bear. When grieving, people become aware of all the things that they will no longer be able to say, including 'sorry'. But if we feel guilty about the climate, what exactly do we feel guilty for? And in what sense? The people of Boston were not the cause of the flood that devastated their town in December 2013. Neither would that flood constitute any form of 'just' consequence for moral failures that operate at a global level. This mismatch between individual acts and collective responsibility haunts the environmental debate and brings complexity to any discussion of guilt and blame applied to the impacts of human behaviour on the natural world. It makes it easy for feelings of guilt either to be displaced into blaming others or internalized into a form of self-condemnation, what Tim Jensen calls 'shame'.[1]

The Christian tradition approaches human guilt not just as an emotion but as a fact of our moral condition. It also recognizes corporate guilt, the possibility that the sins of the few may be visited upon the many. Two 'deadly' sins identified in the Christian tradition seem to be particularly implicated here: greed and sloth. The sin of greed is the sin of allowing what we want to distort our perspective on what we need. The biblical ethic of sufficiency is choked by greed when we refuse to be satisfied with having enough and become intent on getting more. The association with the current ecological crisis is obvious. Over-consumption is one thing, but another is a set of expectations about how far it is reasonable to travel to work or on holiday and when it should be possible to buy tropical fruit in a northern European winter. The sin of sloth is the sin of preferring to do what is easy or expedient rather than what is right. Doing our Christian duty is, Jesus teaches, an easy yoke and a light burden, but it is not *no* burden. Those of us with the capacity to choose display sloth when, for example, we drive a journey that could easily be done by walking

1 Tim Jensen, 2019, *Ecologies of Guilt in Environmental Rhetorics*, Cham, Switzerland: Palgrave Macmillan.

or cycling. Collectively, we display sloth by constructing systems of production and supply that are 'efficient' but whose human and environmental costs are borne by others and elsewhere. (Much of this system construction may feel like hard work, but sloth is not an unwillingness to work, but rather a choice of what is expedient over what is right.) The duty of humanity to tend and steward God's good creation is not conspicuous at the fore-front of our economic policy and management.

So there is real human wrongdoing in evidence. Some of this takes the form of specific individual sins, but there is also a *complicity* apparent in our acceptance of a way of life in which patterns of consumption and waste are so normal as to be invis-ible. The emotion of guilt may align unhelpfully with these specifics. Feeling guilty is not, in Christian terms, expiatory, and self-condemnation is dangerously close to another deadly sin – despair. The point of drawing attention to our sin, in Christian belief and practice, is to lead to repentance, forgiveness and redemption. Unfaced guilt delays healing, yet my experience with the floods in Boston, as in my pastoral practice more generally, has been that facing up to guilt as a real problem with a real solu-tion can lead to real transformation not just of people's emotions but of their subsequent behaviour.

This makes it puzzling that a discussion of sin and forgiveness is not closer to the surface in Christian responses to the climate crisis. These have rightly sought to reaffirm a positive doctrine of creation. Recognizing that (as the Psalmist says) the earth is the Lord's, its fullness and all its people, is certainly important. But that recognition carries with it a call to repentance that is less audible. We have sinned. We have been greedy and slothful. We have consumed more than we needed to, and we have organized our lives around making things easy rather than doing our duty. We have not taken proper care of God's good world. The result is not just environmental damage, but the moral chaos of a great many small sins adding up to one enormous sin, of a terrifying mismatch of actions and their consequences. The metre of water at the base of the tower of Boston Stump was not there because of my personal sin, or even because of my complicity in the sin-fulness of our extravagant way of life. But it may well have been there because of hundreds of millions of small instances of greed and sloth.

I have already said that the Christian tradition offers a definitive response to human guilt. Despite that, guilt is often the emotion that is least well handled in the Church's response to the grieving process. Liturgical confession at a funeral service may not be the best answer, but some space for recognizing the things that have gone wrong is essential. I encounter a general reluctance, even among clergy, to acknowledge these things. Christian ministry to the bereaved requires, then, a delicate balancing act between the comfort of Christian hope and the hard fact of real loss. The same may be true with regard to climate grief. Of all the emotions we experience in our grief – anger, sadness, but also thanksgiving; of all the strategies we adopt for coping with our grief – denial, bargaining, but also celebration; guilt is the hardest to acknowledge. And yet when it comes to the environment it is also a plain fact of our predicament. I wonder whether our present debates about the climate can be read as an expression of a collective grieving process, unacknowledged and therefore disabling, in which denial and bargaining line up in one corner (asserting that things are nowhere near as bad as all that) and do battle with anger and sadness in the other (asserting that everything is awful and there is no hope), with nobody wanting to face up to the guilt. We did this to ourselves, but we would seemingly rather do anything with the pain of that guilt than confess it, repent of the sins that underlie it, and open it up to the healing and redeeming power of God.

I am not an expert in climate science, but as a psychologist and a priest I do recognize the grieving process – what it does to people even when they don't know that they are grieving. In that connection, the Christian faith has something serious and distinctive to offer to the climate crisis; it offers us a way of understanding the guilt, and somewhere to go with it. The cross of Jesus Christ is, for Christians, God's complete and perfect answer to the problem of human sin. It doesn't change things that have already happened, of course. We're stuck with the world as it is, the world as we have made it. But it does set it all in the new and transforming context of resurrection. God can redeem even this.

22

Grief in a Silent Sea

TIM GORDON

If creation reveals the glory of the Lord, then the Great Barrier Reef must be a canonical mainstay.

When you strap on a scuba tank and plunge beneath the waves, you undergo a psychedelic assault on the senses. There are more colours here than you knew existed, painted on to a physical structure more complex than you thought possible. Shoals of brightly coloured fish shimmer in the sunbeams as they dart among clouds of microscopic plankton. Shrimp and crabs scuttle among the branching undergrowth, nonplussed by the frantic battles of territorial damselfish raging around them. A stingray glides on fluttering wings over a patchwork of vibrant corals, as a turtle lifts itself towards the surface with a lazy beat of its flippers. Predatory grouper lurk in the shadows, mouths held open for daring cleaner-fish to swim through their gills and pick morsels off their razor-sharp teeth. Crescent fins slice through the water as sharks cruise effortlessly along the reef crest. Life teems around you, in greater diversity here than anywhere else on earth. Around every corner, behind every outcrop, beneath every overhang, are life forms 'most beautiful and most wonderful';[1] countless additions to this ecological miracle. Previous authors have described this place as being filled with 'thunderclaps of wonder';[2] trying to take it all in at once is overwhelming to the point of breathlessness. Before you know it, you've sucked your

---

1 Darwin, Charles, 1859, *On The Origin of Species by Means of Natural Selection, or, The Preservation of Favoured Races in the Struggle for Life*, London: John Murray.

2 Callum Roberts, 2019, *Reef Life: An Underwater Memoir*, London: Profile Books.

scuba tank empty and you must return 'topside', left spluttering for air and the words to describe all that you've seen.

My work as a marine biologist is to record and understand the sounds of this underwater Eden. Jacques Cousteau once described the sea as a 'silent world', but this could hardly be further from the truth. When we do choose to listen to what is already so visually overwhelming, we discover a whole new dimension. The claw-clicks of thousands of snapping shrimp form an endless crackle, like a backing track that is decorated by the pops, trills, growls and hums of fishes. As I swim through the reef in the early morning, I hear the joyful dawn chorus of its inhabitants, just as you hear birdsong when you walk through a forest. Some of these sounds are heart-warmingly familiar; the chatter of a clownfish family; the whoop of an Ambon damselfish; the purrs of sergeant majors; the buzz of a riled-up dusky farmerfish and perhaps even the far-off songs of whales in the deep. Other sounds are less familiar; whistles and grunts from anonymous singers that pique my curiosity and fill my mind with wonder. Together, this collection of sounds forms a biological symphony that echoes many of the psalms: 'I sing for joy at what your hands have done. How great are your works, LORD'; 'the sea, vast and spacious, teeming with creatures beyond number'; 'LORD, our Lord, how majestic is your name in all the earth!' (Psalm 92.4–5; 104.25; 8.9, NIV). The reef sound rings in my ears, lifting my heart upwards and inspiring me to join in praise of its composer.

Or rather, it used to.

Today, I survey graveyards. My colleagues and I are measuring the fastest rates of destruction ever documented in the 24-million-year history of tropical coral reefs. Ravaged by relentless marine heatwaves, corals around the world are bleaching white, dying and fading to grey. As we descend beneath the waves, we gaze in horror at the wreckage around us. Limestone skeletons stand where reefs once buzzed with life, like tombstones in the haunting emptiness. Shrouds of filamentous algae hang off them like grave clothes. And for the first time, we record a sound that has never before been heard on coral reefs: silence. The underwater symphony has been stopped in its tracks. The bubbles from our exhaled breaths echo around the eerie quiet; a painful reminder

of all that has been lost. We return topside, sombre and speech-
less. Songs of praise turn to silent despair.

A million miles away in space and time, Jesus stood with his
friends in another graveyard. They too were grieving, at the
tomb of Lazarus (John 11.1–44). And despite obvious contextual
differences, Jesus' responses to his grief inspire me to respond
similarly to the destruction I see in our own dying world.

'Jesus wept.' Famously the shortest verse in the Bible, this is
rich with significance. As his friends and followers cried with
anguish at the death of their friend, Jesus shared their tears.
Grief was never academic or distant or small to Jesus; rather,
he grieved himself. In fact, he didn't just weep; he got angry, he
raged, he flipped tables and he screamed (see, for example, Mark
3 and John 2). The message is clear: our grief, anger and distress
in response to the world's suffering are not to be suppressed or
denied. They are feelings that God shared and fully embraced
when he came to earth.

Jesus' graveside anguish is very important to me in my work,
because it gives me the courage to face my own grief. Knowing that Jesus was torn apart by his encounters with death and
suffering teaches me that this isn't a weak response. It isn't
inappropriate or distracting or unhelpful. It's a response that we
share with the creator and redeemer of the world. Grieving can
be frowned upon in scientific institutions; we're told there isn't
space for it in a culture of precision. Outpourings of emotion
are an admission of a loss of control that precludes objectivity.
But Jesus' grief wasn't a loss of control, but a human response
to suffering. When we cry out in hopelessness and despair, Jesus
doesn't sympathize from a distance. He puts an arm around us
and says, 'I know.'

Jesus' actions at Lazarus' tomb went beyond tears, though.
His empathy at the graveside was poignant, but it didn't solve
the problem; Jesus came to Lazarus' grave to do more than just
mourn. As well as crying with his friends, Jesus pointed them
towards hope. Remarkably, he chose this moment of darkest
grief to make the most hopeful statement in the whole Gospel:
'I am the resurrection and the life.' This promise is a powerful

statement of authority and comfort, delivered in the depths of suffering and despair. There is joy after weeping. Though we walk in darkness today, there will be redemption tomorrow. This cornerstone of Christian faith, that God came into the world to save it, rings loudest when our grief is at its darkest.

This hope in the darkness was true when Jesus' followers stood at the tomb of their friend, and it is true when I swim through the wrecked remains of the once-Great Barrier Reef. The Bible's salvation narrative is clear: God made all things and will redeem all things, 'whether things on earth or things in heaven' (Colossians 1.20, NIV). John's Revelation vision of 'a new heaven and a new earth' (Revelation 21.1, NIV). speaks not of novelty but of renewal; the word used is *kainos*, which is the same word used by Paul to describe ourselves as made new when we become Christians (Ephesians 4.24). The fact that creation is wrapped up within the resurrection promise is important; redemption is promised for the natural world in the same way that it was promised for Lazarus and is promised for all of us. In the midst of devastation, the almost-impossibly wonderful truth remains for all things: Jesus is the resurrection and the life.

But holding on to this hope is difficult. In the overwhelming hurt of the moment, nebulous images of resurrection are hard to cling to; the almost impossible becomes scarcely believable. Future redemption can be of little comfort in the face of dead friends, and Martha's knowledge that her brother would rise again 'in the resurrection at the last day' didn't make the pain of losing him any less real. In the same way, knowing that creation will eventually be restored doesn't take the sting out of watching the world's coral reefs crumble to pieces. For me, this is why Jesus' action at Lazarus' tomb means so much. While his friends and followers couldn't see further than the stench of the rotting corpse, Jesus could. Calling on those around him to roll away the tombstone, he was adamant that 'If you believe, you will see the glory of God'. His responses to suffering weren't empty eschatological escapism; there was never any naive, arm-waving 'Suffering hurts now, but it's only temporary and it'll be OK in the end because you'll go to heaven and leave all of this behind'. The incarnate Jesus who cried with people on earth doesn't deal in pious indifference. Instead, he called his disciples to act with him, in the midst of the painful here-and-now. Throughout his life, Jesus fed the hungry and healed the sick, praying 'Your will be done on earth as it is in heaven'. In doing so, he didn't remove all of suffering from the world immediately – disease is still rampant, injustice still pervades and people still suffer, curse and cry today. But he did point to a better future.

As a marine biologist, this reminds me that my small actions are far from worthless. I may not be able to bring dead corals back to life, regrow the Great Barrier Reef or undo the ghastly results of my surveys. The damage is too extensive. But I can work to protect what still remains, replace some of what has been lost, and make active changes to protect people and environments around the world. It won't remove environmental destruction from the planet entirely, but it will make a difference where I am and point to a better future. Just as Jesus brought God's love to a small corner of Palestine, I can bring healing to small corners of the world today. In their own way, both point to an ultimate resurrection.

Jesus never scuba-dived on a dying Great Barrier Reef. He never saw the colours fade, the architecture collapse and the symphony silenced. But I think his words and actions at Lazarus' tomb show us how he might respond to today's environmental crises. If, while on earth, Jesus had seen the riches of creation reduced to a rubble field, he surely would have wept with us for its loss. He surely would have pointed us to its future redemption. And he surely would have used this as motivation to protect all that still remains of the planet's wonders.

'I am the resurrection and the life,' said Jesus, as his cheeks shone with tears. One day, the sea will sing again.

23

Grieving the Land in Northern Namibia

NANGULA EVA-LIISA KATHINDI

'The earth is the LORD's and all that is in it, the world, and those who live in it' (Psalm 24.1, NRSV). Namibia's climate is mostly subtropical; a desert climate characterized by great differences in day- and night-time temperatures. It has a low rainfall and over-all low humidity. In Namibia we experience winter and summer at opposite times to Europe and North America, and they correspond to the dry and wet seasons.

It is in this context that I speak about the challenges our country faces with climate change. As far as I can remember, drought has always been part of our lives. There was hardly a year when farmers were not concerned about their crops and how to save their animals from dying from hunger and lack of water. The year 2019 has been characterized by the worst drought. Most of Namibia did not receive much rain for grazing and for people to grow crops. Only a few areas in the northern part of the country (areas of Kavango and Zambezi) have been able to harvest some crops. Rural church communities could not celebrate the usual harvest thanksgiving due to the lack of their own produce. They had to buy goods from local grocers for thanksgiving services.

Mr Tomas Andreas Nakanyala is a cattle farmer in Iikokola village, Onayena Constituency in the Oshikoto region. Mr Nakanyala is 74 years old and has been farming for the past 40 years. He concluded that the 2019 drought has been the worst drought. He has 14 members in his family and since they could not produce any food due to lack of rain he spent N$15,000 to buy food and pay for water and electricity.

Historically some men in my culture have succumbed to death because of stress from heavy loss of their cattle. Doctors and chaplains from our hospitals have shared experiences of admitted male patients enumerating their dead cattle instead of stating bodily ailments. Counselling such patients has been very challenging. In times of drought it is necessary for clergy to give counselling to those who find it difficult to cope. Keeping cattle for Oshiwambo- and Otjiherero-speaking people is cultural pride as it has been passed on from generation to generation. As development has brought about many changes, this cultural heritage also has to accommodate change, especially the climate grief to which we are now exposed.

The African continent is nicknamed the 'Mother Continent' as it is the oldest inhabited continent on earth. It is believed that humans and human ancestors lived in Africa for more than 5 million years. In Africa, many people's livelihood and existence still depend on the land. Most of our rural communities still depend on the land and rain to produce food and make a living. For Africans, land is everything. Depriving a person of land means robbing them of their personhood, existence and identity – in other words, their full humanity. Land belongs to the living, the dead and the unborn, making it inalienable. In most of Africa, land lies at the heart of social, cultural, political and economic life where agriculture, natural resources and other land-based activities are fundamental to livelihoods, food security, income and employment.

Access to land means having food for the family, income and even a small-scale business venture in the community. Without land, a person will feel as if he or she does not have a sense of belonging or is not fully human:

African land laws debunk the idea of ownership ... African land tenure is not based on ownership but on use and access. Since Africans have common rights to land, communal rights override individual rights, which are subsumed to the overall communal good.[1]

However, it becomes challenging to have access to land when you cannot produce anything on it or even save your animals due to lack of water and grass. Even with the limited government support in introducing seeds for drought-resistant crops to subsistence farmers, they still struggle to make ends meet.

Ms Rakkel Mateus is a 56-year-old crop and livestock farmer from Iikokola Village, Onayena constituency in the Oshikoto region. Ms Mateus has been farming for the past 27 years and keeps cattle and goats. Her crops are mahangu, sorghum and beans. She believes that the drought of 2019 has been the worst of all the droughts she has experienced so far. Her area was terribly affected by the drought – there was no grass and water in the area for the animals to feed. She attempted six times to plant but completely failed to harvest any crop for her family of seven. Her family survived on the mahangu she kept from the previous harvest. She was lucky to have some mahangu left over, unlike many families who did not have any. She spent about N$9,000 for four months to buy other food for the family.

As a strategy to save some of her cattle from drought, she gave two cattle to her uncle who lives in an area where there was grass and water. The two cattle survived the drought; unfortunately she lost 29 of her 39 cattle. Most cattle died of plastic bags which they consumed due to lack of grazing. She spent N$7,000 on feed, water and vaccines for animals.

The effect of the drought on the environment has been felt in the extremely hot temperatures during the summer months.

New land laws have improved the process of land redistribution in most of the African communities. However, there are still communities where access to land is still gender-based, where most of

---

1 Kenneth Tafira, 2015, 'Why Land Evokes Such Deep Emotions in Africa', *The Conversation*, 27 May, https://theconversation.com/why-land-evokes-such-deep-emotions-in-africa-42125, accessed 12/06/20.

the land is still owned by men, and women face discrimination. Most of the women have access to land through marriage and even when their husbands have died there is still a threat of it being taken away – even by their sisters-in-law. Women fighting for survival even turn on each other, despite facing the same predicament when their husbands die. Justice still needs to be sought in this area so that women can also enjoy their rights to land.

Ecumenical prayers for rain have been organized across all churches, especially in the breadbasket of the country. This act of faith is usually the practice that people rely on for God's mercy to give them rain.

So Moses cried out to the LORD, 'What shall I do with this people? They are almost ready to stone me.' The LORD said to Moses, 'Go on ahead of the people, and take some of the elders of Israel with you; take in your hand the staff with which you struck the Nile, and go. I will be standing there in front of you on the rock at Horeb. Strike the rock, and water will come out of it, so that the people may drink.' (Exodus 17.4–6, NRSV)

Namibians have experienced many challenges in the past, which have brought them closer to God through prayer, like the struggle for independence and freedom from the system of apartheid by the RSA government. The challenge of drought also forces people to come closer to God and to one another. When the drought persisted, people stepped up their prayers at family, local parish and national levels. Like the Israelites, when they needed water in the desert, people turned to God for help.

To Namibians, it was very clear that help was not coming from elsewhere: God was their only hope when it comes to the drought and beyond. Christians reached out to one another to pray together instead of remaining in their own churches. Prayer gatherings gave people hope to continue trusting God and look forward to the end of the drought. Christians used the time of prayer to confess their sins and got close to God. Ideas on how to deal with the drought were shared, for example how to grow animal feed using little water and still succeed (such as using a hydroponics system to cultivate plants without using soil). This method helped many farmers to grow animal feed and save their animals.

As a priest, it was difficult to see the suffering of the people and animals, and the only thing I could do was to pray and practise the ministry of presence. I also had to think about the context in which I was preaching the gospel to God's people. I introduced parishes in my archdeaconry to the programme Green Anglicans – the Anglican Church of Southern Africa's Environmental Network (ACSA-EN) – with the aim of supporting churches and dioceses to fulfil God's call to be earth-keepers and to care for creation. My sermons touched on themes of how to care for and protect the environment, that is, God's creation. I taught the importance of collecting plastics and the damage they cause when consumed by animals, and the pollution to our water reservoirs, rivers and the sea. The drought taught us how to save and preserve water at home and in the community.

> Mr Nakanyala had 36 head of cattle before the drought. He decided to move them to an area where he thought they would be safe, about 100 km away from his village. He spent about N$6,000 on transport, feed, water and vaccines. He lost 28 of the 36 cattle. The lesson Mr Nakanyala learned from the drought experience is that he will always keep animal feed for a dry season. He also concluded that it is better to maintain a small number of cattle, in order to manage the feed, water and vaccines.

The drought challenged me to appreciate the gift of God's resources to us, his people. The threat of plastic pollution and its negative effects on the fish and other marine animals is very concerning. I also made a commitment to continue gardening and show the integrity of producing what we consume to other Christians. We understood the reality that we live in a semi-desert country and need to take care of what God has given us. Our survival and that of God's creation depends sorely on how we manage these endowments. We have learnt useful lessons that prepared us even if we have to face another drought in the future.

It is natural for people in my community to express their grief to God through poems, songs and storytelling. The poems, songs and stories are shared in services and other community gatherings and even on social media. The same happens when thanksgiving is expressed towards God for God's blessings. Climate grief is also expressed through songs sung by various choirs, Sunday school children, youth groups, men's and women's Bible study groups. The Church encourages Bible study and prayer groups to engage the issue of climate grief. But now our grief must help us move from stories and songs to defending the rights of God's children.

The Church represents more than 90 per cent of our citizens and needs to reach out to her communities and see how the situation of land is affecting the people. The Church needs to continue to be the voice of the voiceless even on the issue of land. The majority of Namibians, especially women, are still in need of land. The Church must represent the people's needs to the government, pressuring them to pass laws that give citizens access to this inalienable resource. It is therefore high time that the question of land and the people be taken up as a point of discussion in the Church. The issue of land and the people from the biblical point of view needs further engagement as a contribution of the Church to society. Communities need to be mobilized for people to understand their land rights and pursue those rights. The time has come for the light of understanding to shine on the land rights of every Namibian. The Church is the right institution to make this contribution to society. This will also give deeper meaning to Psalm 24.1: 'The earth is the LORD's and all that is in it, the world, and those who live in it.'

24

Colour

AZARIAH FRANCE-WILLIAMS

Gather the women of colour
then scatter their wisdom
like seeds
may white soil incubate
and accommodate their words
not just tolerate, pretend you've heard.
And may their words become flesh and live
and breathe and walk amongst us.

PART 3

As It Will Be

25

The Sea and the Poor in the Indonesian Archipelago

ELIA MAGGANG

Indonesian Archipelago

Indonesia is the largest archipelagic state in the world, consisting of more than 17,000 islands, of which around 7,000 islands are inhabited by more than 260 million people.[1] Two-thirds of its area is the sea (6.3 million square kilometres), with 99,093km of coastline.[2] Its vast marine ecology benefits not only Indonesia but the whole earth: Indonesia is the home of the largest mangroves (22.6 per cent)[3] and second-largest coral reefs (16 per cent)[4] on this blue planet. Around 60 per cent of the coral triangle area is located in the eastern part of Indonesia, making it rich with marine biodiversity. Those thousand islands also speak of social diversity. There are 1,300 ethnic groups,[5] over 700 different

---

1 John David Legge et al., 'Indonesia', *Encyclopædia Britannica*, www.britannica.com/place/Indonesia, accessed 15/07/2020.

2 Subandono Diposaptono, 2017, *Membangun Poros Maritim Dunia Dalam Perspektif Tata Ruang Laut* (Developing the Global Maritime Fulcrum in the Sea Spatial Planning Perspective), Jakarta: Kementerian Kelautan dan Perikanan, p. 27.

3 C. Giri et al., 2011, 'Status and Distribution of Mangrove Forests of the World Using Earth Observation Satellite Data', *Global Ecology and Biogeography* 20(1), p. 157.

4 Lauretta Burke et al., 2013, *Reefs at Risk Revisited in the Coral Triangle*, Washington, DC: World Resources Institute, p. 26.

5 Sarah Yuniari, 2016, 'Unity in Diversity: Indonesia's Six Largest Ethnic Groups', *Jakarta Globe*, https://jakartaglobe.id/culture/unity-diversity-indonesias-six-largest-ethnic-groups/, accessed 15/07/2020.

native languages[6] and hundreds of religions (six national religions: Islam, Christianity (Protestant and Roman Catholic), Hinduism, Buddhism and Confucianism – and the local religions) – all are connected by the sea to be and live as Indonesia.

These ecological and social dimensions are intertwined in maritime cultures. Human encounters with the sea generate a particular way of life. For the Indonesian Archipelago, climate change is a severe threat to the sea and, consequently, for those whose life is dependent on the sea. For the coastal people of the eastern part of the archipelago, in particular, the sea is essential as their food and livelihood come from the sea. For the poor, the sea looks after them by providing nutritious food. The destruction of life in the sea is also the destruction of life in the community.[7]

The sea feeds the poor

In my hometown of Kupang, West Timor, the sea is significant not only because it gives fresh fish for us every day but most importantly the sea feeds the poor. For these communities, the seafood (aquatic plants and animals), which can be collected/caught directly from the sea during the low tide, is the food for the poor. This traditional practice is intentional as those considered as the poor do not have and cannot afford a boat and adequate fishing equipment. In the community of Pantai Rote in Semau Island, for instance, the poor people are regarded with two local expressions that usually emerge in traditional poetry. They are *ina falu* (widows) and *ana mak* (orphans). Their food comes directly from the sea and, therefore, their life is dependent on the sea. With traditional and simple equipment, *ina falu* and

---

6 Benjamiń Elisha Sawe, 2017, 'What Languages are Spoken in Indonesia?', WorldAtlas, www.worldatlas.com/articles/what-languages-are-spoken-in-indonesia.html, accessed 15/07/2020.

7 Elia Maggang, 2020, 'Menampakkan Corak Biru Kekristenan Indonesia' (To Display the Blue Hues of Indonesian Christianity), *Indonesian Journal of Theology* 7(2), pp. 162–88, p. 170.

ana mak collect small fish, crabs, octopuses, seaweeds and other kinds of seafood from the sea during the low tide twice a day.[8]

This practice is the way coastal societies look after the poor, based on their encounter with the sea with all its potentials for life. Those in poverty are empowered as they do not ask for food, but look for food. The people in the communities acknowledge the sea as the one feeding the poor with nutritious food, while those who have better fishing equipment look for the food in other areas. And the poor recognize that the sea is a crucial source of their life.

That kind of Indonesian maritime culture portrays the significant role of the sea with its intrinsic value in the community of creation. As Elizabeth A. Johnson writes, each part of God's creation has an intrinsic value which supports our common life.[9] The sea and all its living creatures contribute food, oxygen, water through the hydrological system, keep the balance of temperature, and so on. Sylvia Earle is correct to say that the ocean is the cornerstone of life on this blue planet.[10] The sea, in this regard, is a participant in the community of creation. The sea is not defined by the ways humans exploit it as an object. It is a subject that contributes to the whole life of God's creation, including human life. As Winston Halapua says, the waves of the oceans breaking over reefs and embracing the coastlines speak of God's love that gives life without ceasing.[11] In the maritime culture of Indonesia, which is a part of the community of creation, a form of the intrinsic value of the sea is demonstrated by feeding the poor.

When I consider maritime culture in the framework of the community of creation, it resonates with the feeding narratives

---

8 Tom Therik, 1997, 'Meramu Makanan Dari Laut: Kearifan Masyarakat Pantai Rote Di Semau' (Collecting Seafood from the Sea: Local Wisdom of Pantai Rote Society in Semau), *Setia* 1, pp. 76–91.

9 Elizabeth A. Johnson, 2014, *Ask the Beasts: Darwin and the God of Love*, London: Bloomsbury, p. 268.

10 Sylvia Earle, 2016, 'Protect the Ocean, Protect Ourselves', in Marcha Johnson and Amanda Bayley (eds), *Coastal Change, Ocean Conservation and Resilient Communities*, Cham: Springer International Publishing, p. 156.

11 Winston Halapua, 2008, *Waves of God's Embrace*, Norwich: Canterbury Press, pp. 93–5.

of Jesus as recorded in the Gospels. Jesus feeds the multitude not only with loaves but also fishes. Jesus was part of a maritime community: the inland water of Galilee where the fishes were taken is a lake, yet Matthew, Mark and John consistently use the Greek word for 'sea'. Among Jesus' disciples were those who experienced the fishing industry under the Roman Empire's economic system – as fishermen and tax collector.[12] For the Galileans, their food came from the inland water. For the coastal communities in the Indonesian Archipelago, it comes from the sea. The two fish from the inland water of Galilee were used by Jesus to feed thousands of hungry people, the poor. Jesus invites the inland water of Galilee to participate in the community of creation by feeding the poor.

By the work of the Spirit, God also lets the sea participate in the community of creation by feeding the poor in Kupang and other coastal communities in the Indonesian Archipelago. The maritime culture in these places is the work of the Spirit who dwells and brings life to each edge of this planet. As for where the Spirit is, there life is, says St Ambrosius.[13] Through the sea, its existence and potential, the Spirit shapes the maritime communities with a particular view and practice for the common life of all as their culture. As Jesus commanded the disciples to feed the poor and invite the participation of the inland water of Galilee, the Spirit's movement in the maritime communities of the Indonesian Archipelago 'commands' the people to 'let' the sea feed the poor.

---

12 See K. C. Hanson, 1999, 'The Galilean Fishing Economy and the Jesus Tradition', *Biblical Theology Bulletin* 27(3), pp. 99–111, and John S. Kloppenborg, 2018, 'Jesus, Fishermen and Tax Collectors: Papyrology and Construction of the Ancient Economy of Roman Palestine', *Ephemerides Theologicae Lovanienses* 94(4), pp. 571–99.

13 Cited in Sigurd Bergmann, 2019, 'The Spirit and Climate Change', in Ernst M. Conradie and Hilda P. Koster (eds), *T&T Clark Handbook of Christian Theology and Climate Change*, London: Bloomsbury, p. 497.

The groaning sea: suffering and hope

For the sea to feed the poor in the maritime culture mentioned above, the conditions of ecosystems in the shallow sea is decisive. The average temperature is crucial for aquatic animals and plants. If the ecosystem is damaged, it will affect the availability of seafood for the poor and the participation of the sea in the community of creation.

This is no longer an 'if': climate change is destabilizing the sea temperature and gradually destroying the coral reefs. Climate change hinders the vulnerable sea from participating in the community of creation, forcing the sea to groan altogether with the rest of creation. The groaning sea is none other than the impact of human sin.[14] But, while all humans sin, this sin against the sea is not committed by poor people. It is those in power who have sinned against the sea and the poor.

The sea is groaning because the powerful act of climate change is too difficult to solve. I wish the solutions were dependent on the poor. It is not rocket science to explain to the poor the significance of coral reefs, and then see behaviour change. Local fishers look after the coral reefs by not practising destructive fishing such as blast fishing, potassium fishing, and so on. Yet, what can they do if the coral reefs are damaged, or the sea temperature is destabilized by climate change? Climate change is beyond the capacity of the poor or the artisanal fishers in the Indonesian Archipelago. They have no way other than to suffer from what they do not do. The intrinsic value of the sea is denied, and the people the sea looks after severely threatened. The maritime culture in which the sea is in a special relationship with the poor is broken by climate change. The sea is groaning like a mother who suffers from not being able to feed her children. The sea is groaning as it is hindered from feeding the *ina falu* and *ana mak*.

However, beneath its groan, the sea is eagerly longing for liberation from climate change. It is not an empty groan, but a certain hope for the transformation of all things.[15] Jesus' work

---

14 See Richard Bauckham, 2010, *Bible and Ecology: Rediscovering the Community of Creation*, London: Darton, Longman and Todd, pp. 95–101.
15 Bauckham, *Bible and Ecology*, p. 101.

of feeding the poor with the two fish from the 'Sea' of Galilee is a sign of hope. Jesus liberates the Sea of Galilee from the Roman Empire's exploitative and oppressive economic system which only benefited those in power. Raj Nadella asserts that Jesus resists this Roman centripetal movement of resources with the feeding narrative, which demonstrates the centrifugal movement of resource – an economy of sharing.[16] More than that, Jesus actually restores the participation of the Sea of Galilee in the community of creation. The Lord of the sea (Mark 4.35–41) is bringing back the Sea of Galilee to its intrinsic value, one that feeds the poor. This is a foretaste of the kingdom of God to come, which is the hope of the sea for liberation from climate change.

Like Simon Peter and his fellows in the feeding narrative, Jesus' disciples today are commanded to feed the poor by the help of the Spirit. As disciples we are called to participate in God's work of restoring the intrinsic value of the sea – to let the sea once again feed *ina falu* and *ana mak*.

Religion that is pure and undefiled before God, the Father, is this: to care for orphans and widows in their distress, and to keep oneself unstained by the world. (James 1.27, NRSV)

16 Raj Nadella, 2016, 'The Two Banquets: Mark's Vision of Anti-Imperial Economics', *Interpretation* 70(2), pp. 173–5.

26

The Knotted Conscience of Privilege

DAVID BENJAMIN BLOWER

Fifty per cent of global emissions are caused by the richest 10 per cent of the world's population.[1] For some of us, the road to grief is knotted with guilt.

Guilt avoidance is a mainstream political energy in the Global North today. Denial from some of the biggest carbon emitters. Beefed-up borders to resist the mass movements of people that have already begun: a move that locates the problem outside, with other people and not with ourselves. These are the marks of a system that doesn't want to die, and doesn't want to admit that it knows what everybody knows. Power always resists a recognition of how much outsourced death makes our own exceptional life possible.

In talking among people of faith and privilege about climate collapse and culpability, I began to notice a recurring trope: things are getting bad. So bad that Jesus must surely come back soon. I began to wonder if there wasn't a thread of exceptionalism in this assumption too. Jesus didn't return when European settlers caused the death of more than 50 million Native Americans, or the enslavement of 12 million Africans, or the murder of 7 million Jewish men, women and children. Why are we so sure the Messiah will return as soon as we see a catastrophe that might reach even us? Why is ours more important than anyone else's? What if we are the early Church, and the world will have to limp on for ages after what we do to it?

---

1 Timothy Gore, 2015, *Extreme Carbon Inequality*, Oxfam. Available from https://oi-files-d8-prod.s3.eu-west-2.amazonaws.com/s3fs-public/file_attach ments/mb-extreme-carbon-inequality-021215-en.pdf, accessed 18/08/2020.

And honestly, with what emotional map do we process this? Human history has never encountered, much less caused, the possibility of so much death. No creature in earth's natural history has done what we are now doing, nor had the consciousness to contemplate it.

I was fascinated by Timothy Morton's exploration of how journeying through guilt and dread leads us out into a story much bigger than our own exceptionalism, and even bigger than our guilt. 'We are beginning to trust the tactic of not waking ourselves up from the nightmare, but allowing ourselves to fall further into it, beyond horror,' he says.[2] When we find ourselves powerless to atone for ourselves and stunned by the possible scale of the wreckage, maybe we'll finally zoom out into deep time: into a story bigger than the world of human beings, and much bigger than the strange world of the richest 10 per cent.

A while ago I learned the etymology of the word 'world': from Germanic languages, *wer-auld*, meaning human-age. Not so much the earth itself, as an age of life upon it. Contemplating a dying world, and our own culpability, leads on to thinking about the world that will come after. Maybe there will be humans, and maybe not. But there will certainly be life. And, of course, there was a world *before*; before humans. Suddenly the mere fact of our existence presents itself as it is: as miracle and gift. A tragicomedy. Unfinished and not without hope, but not a thing can we make guarantees for either. Maybe God can, but we can't.

These two poems were written towards a grief that might guide even the most culpable of us to gratitude, stunned wonder and, in proportion to that wonder, change.

The Wall

We all walk into the future backwards
Because the past is our only reference
And only rarely does the present demand
That we turn and refer to what's stood there ahead of us

---

2 Timothy Morton, 2018, *Being Ecological*, London: Pelican.

And when the future demands that we turn and behold
We will confound it, and say, 'no'
And any who turn and say what they see
We will no longer break bread with these

For if we must hit the wall
It is our wish to do so unknowingly
Can we hope for any better ending than this?

If only it were so, but we do know
We can smell it and we can feel it in our bones
And to suspend our knowing unknowing
We go and hang what we know on the tired bones of those

Scapegoat the wretched of the earth
For the judgement that we piled against ourselves
And all before creation gives birth to the new things we
    cannot imagine
Nor should we have any right to taste them

And then she will take back from us
All her stolen sabbath's rest
We will say on that holy day
Amen and yes.

The Floor

And then shall we fall through all our troubled thoughts
And awaken to panic guilt and dread
And then shall we fall through the floor once more
And then into tears and laughter instead

And wonder and sorrow over everything that is
In ecstatic clarity and madness
And every thread of this dread comedy of foolishness
That we really existed and we really did this

And nothing can be undone
Only tended and forgiven

And then shall we open our small clenched fists
And hold out palms of powerless thankfulness
For everything that we received was gift
And so much love and wonder in our midst

And finally stand we all in defeated awe
At everything was and is and shall be evermore.

27

Reconciliation: Lament and Hope

VICTORIA MARIE

Vancouver, British Columbia, is surrounded by water on three sides. It is bounded by Burrard Inlet to the north, the Fraser River to the south, and the Strait of Georgia, to the west, is shielded from the Pacific Ocean by Vancouver Island. Vancouver is 3,923 kilometres, as the crow flies from Brooklyn, New York, where I was born and raised. It is a city built on the stolen lands of the Tsleil-Watuth, Squamish and Musqueam First Nations, who live on Indian Reserves in and around the city. Most indigenous nations in British Columbia have never signed a treaty with Canada or ceded their lands.

The ascendency of xenophobic sentiments and lack of government responses to clear evidence of impending climate disaster make it a struggle to keep hope alive. I can't help but see that racism and apathy towards climate change intersect. I worry about the fate of peoples of colour and indigenous peoples, and the numerous species that are most impacted by climate change inaction. It is hard to instil hope in the worship community that I lead, when at times I am close to despair. The members of the small congregation I lead are all of European descent, making it difficult to share the sorrow and angst I feel about environmental racism and climate change, while trying to encourage activism rather than apathy.

Oil spills, grey smoke-filled skies from fires ravaging the interior of British Columbia, pipelines and the destruction caused by their construction feel overwhelming. Climate change is now beginning to negatively affect British Columbia's western red cedar trees. These trees have been used by indigenous peoples in British Columbia for thousands of years in sustainable ways.

Before becoming a priest, I was a member of a Franciscan order of nuns for 15 years and steeped in the Franciscan emphasis on the integrity of creation. In his Canticle of Creation, St Francis of Assisi, founder of the Franciscan orders, addresses the sun, moon and elements as Brother and Sister, the earth as Mother, and ends the Canticle with 'Be praised my Lord for all your creation serving you joyfully'. Similarly, St Bonaventure (1221–74), a Franciscan theologian and philosopher, suggests that in every element of creation there are traces in which we can see God, and 'the invisible God, and the brightness of His glory, and the Image of His substance, exists everywhere'.[1] Building on this, Blessed John Duns Scotus developed the idea of *haecceitas*, which could be translated as 'this-ness'. This concept suggests, for example, that God doesn't just love roses; God loves each individual rose. God doesn't just love a species, but each individual in that species.

This Franciscan view of creation demands that I see earth and all its elements, flora and fauna with the understanding that all are my siblings. It broadens my view of what it means when I read, 'Those who say, "I love God", and hate their brothers or sisters, are liars; for those who do not love a brother or sister whom they have seen, cannot love God whom they have not seen' (1 John 4.20, NRSV). I empathize with my indigenous siblings as a racialized other myself. As a self-healing process, I try to internalize the lesson of 1 John 4.20, so that I can love all of my siblings because I recognize that all are my siblings. I am strengthened and motivated by a Franciscan spiritual lens.

The most important thing for Francis was to follow Christ in the ways of love, poverty and peace. During the madness of the Crusades, when popes were calling all Christians to conquer the Holy Lands and destroy the non-Christians they encountered, Francis went on a different crusade, one of peace-making. Francis crossed paths with Malek al-Kamil, the Sultan of Egypt, who then held Francis captive. During his captivity, the Sultan and Francis developed respect for each other, leading to Francis'

---

1 St Bonaventure, *Works of Bonaventure: Journey of the Mind To God – The Triple Way, or, Love Enkindled – The Tree of Life – The Mystical Vine – On the Perfection of Life, Addressed to Sisters*, Colchis Books, Kindle edition, location 291.

release. Contrary to the prevailing sentiments of the time, St Francis risked his life to bring peace between Christians and Muslims. Through Francis' example, I learned that the work of reconciliation requires conquering and overcoming fear and apathy to keep working for change. Modern-day Franciscans follow Francis' example. They recognize unjust structures and call them to peace and reconciliation through non-violent protest and civil disobedience. The situation in Canada, especially British Columbia, calls me to join with those working for policies that earnestly address climate change and reconciliation with indigenous peoples.

Canada was one of the last three nations to sign the UN Declaration on the Rights of Indigenous Peoples (UNDRIP). As a signatory nation, Canada has agreed to adopt and respect the principle of free, prior and informed consent of indigenous peoples in all matters covered by their specific rights and to obtain their 'free, prior and informed consent when the preservation of their cultural resources, especially those associated with their way of life'. By approving the Kinder Morgan pipeline, Canada violated this principle with regard to members of the Tsleil-Waututh and other coastal First Nations of British Columbia. This makes continued pipeline preparation and building activities violations of UNDRIP.

Canada and Kinder Morgan act with impunity sanctioned by apathy. However, apathy is not a universal trait and people protest against the pipeline. During 2017 and 2018, I was one of the thousands of people who regularly stood with local indigenous people and their allies to protest peacefully outside the gates of the Kinder Morgan (now Trans Mountain) pipeline terminal in Burnaby, a suburb of Vancouver. In response, the company sought and received an injunction to curb the protests.

During one of the protests, I saw an eagles' nest that had been encased by a metal cage. The cage prevented the eagles from tending their eggs. Each time I saw it was like a hammer to the heart. I learned that the Northeast Pacific southern resident population of killer whales were being harmed by the sound of the underwater heavy machinery used in the pipeline project. Early in 2018, I received a second cancer diagnosis and would have to have surgery. These things made it impossible to continue standing on the sidelines. I sat at the gates with four other faith leaders, refusing to move, and was arrested. Over 200 people who support the indigenous land and coast defenders by peacefully protesting the Trans Mountain pipeline have been arrested and – almost without exception – found guilty.

Contrary to a decision by the Supreme Court of Canada, the federal and provincial governments have granted Coastal GasLink permission to build a pipeline through Wet'suwet'en territory in northern British Columbia. The Wet'suwet'en land defenders of Unis'tot'en and Gidimt'en have set up blockades to prevent work on the pipeline. The government response is the RCMP Community Industry Response Group, a militarized section of the Royal Canadian Mounted police. They are prepared to shoot indigenous land defenders blockading construction of this pipeline on their own unceded land.[2] Indigenous groups across Canada have put up railway blockades in solidarity with the Wet'suwet'en against the current RCMP actions at Unis'tot'en. The Wet'suwet'en hereditary chiefs have offered to meet with the government and company officials once the RCWP have left their lands. The RCMP remain.

It appears that reconciliation with indigenous Canadians and the earth has become a criminal offence. When reconciliation becomes meaningful action, that is, goes beyond mere words, it threatens the powers – and they react. Injunctions against peaceful protest are the weapons of choice. Violations of the UN Declaration on the Rights of Indigenous Peoples, the US Eagle Act and the British Columbia Wildlife Act are committed with impunity.

Psalm 98 tells us that the sea and all that fills it, the earth and all those who live in it, are included in the household of God. Therefore, when Jesus says, 'This is my commandment, that you love one another as I have loved you. No one has greater

2 Jaskiran Dhillon and Will Parrish, 2019, 'Exclusive: Canada Police Prepared to Shoot Indigenous Activists, Documents Show', *The Guardian*, 20 December, www.theguardian.com/world/2019/dec/20/canada-indigenous-land-defenders-police-documents?utm_term=Autofeed&CMP=twt_gu&utm_medium=&utm_source=Twitter#Echobox=1576840462, accessed 27/02/20.

love than this, to lay down one's life for one's friends. You are my friends if you do what I command you', Jesus is making an inclusive statement. Our response as faith leaders was not just a political action, but an act of inclusive gospel love.

The situation in British Columbia calls for a response. Why do we respond? Our faith demands it. We believe reconciliation is not an event. Rather, it is a process. Reconciliation is more than an apology: it is the process of building relationships of mutual respect and mutual trust.

We seek reconciliation with all life. When we say we believe in the sanctity of all life, that includes non-human life: the creatures of the sea and the birds of the air. It also includes human livelihood. Overriding it all is the desire to follow Jesus' command to love. That is why at the gates of Westbridge Marine Terminal we prayed for justice for our indigenous brothers and sisters and for Kinder Morgan workers; we prayed for the eagle pair evicted from their home. We prayed for the earth and her waters. That day, we joined the growing number of people arrested for living into reconciliation. Undeterred, and fighting against apathy and despair, our peaceful protests will continue. We believe, like Martin Luther King Jr, that 'the arc of the moral universe is long, but it bends toward justice'. So, motivated by gospel faith and love, we continue to work to make reconciliation a generally accepted reality.

28

Strange Futures

OANA MARIAN

My dream is not of human rights and inclusion into an exhausted colonial order. My dream is an electric hymn sung by gut bacteria ... of cell transfers that queer sources, unsettle originals, and disturb the idea that identity is coherent or articulable. My dream is of the Anthropocene, entangled bodies, and the pleasures of never arriving.[1]

I embraced queerness and began studying Christian theology at around the same time, in 2014. When I enter Christian spaces created especially for queer people, it becomes obvious to me that I am much more 'out' about being queer than I am about the forms of faith I practise. There are people who preserve a wild, unruly space within the parameters of Christian identity, but rejection within my family on the basis of my queerness came from a very different interpretation of Christianity, similar to interpretations of Christianity that have historically plundered land and people and imaginations, and that bear no minor responsibility for the ecological disasters we face now. In the face of this, the most appropriate human responses are also the ones to which many of us are most resistant: grief, atonement, repair, humility – and, if we allow ourselves those, then also wonder, compassion, joy, gratitude, praise.

In my thirty-fifth year, in 2014, I had what I can only imprecisely describe as a conversion experience, not a new call to faith,

---

1 Bayo Akomolafe, 'When You Meet the Monster, Anoint Its Feet', *Emergence Magazine*, https://emergencemagazine.org/story/when-you-meet-the-monster/, accessed 27/08/20.

but an identity-changing awakening to impending ecological disaster. This happened in the midst of significant personal upheaval, among which the death of a lifelong friend and the (not unexpected, but still devastating) rejection by a parent after I met the woman I would end up marrying. Falling in love, as much as losing loved ones, displaces, even annihilates, significant parts of the self. Maybe this is, as the theologian John Zizioulas has suggested, in order to make room for the other. In any case, this word – annihilation – best describes my preoccupation during that time. It is one thing to be informed about greenhouse gas emissions, ocean acidification, accelerating rates of extinction, and another thing altogether to *know*, to metabolize, the disaster within one's body, through which all experience is mediated. And, while grief and joy are not mutually exclusive, this story must be entered through the grief door.

The catalyst for this awakening was a *Guardian* article about the text *Limit to Growth*, written by MIT researchers for an international think tank, in 1972. On 1 September 2014, the headline read, 'Four decades after the book was published, *Limit to Growth*'s forecasts have been vindicated by new Australian research. Expect the early stages of global collapse to start appearing soon'. More affecting than the article itself was a graph that showed the 1972 data lines for industrial output per capita, global pollution, food per capita, non-renewable resources remaining, services per capita, and global population and, alongside them, that same data observed between 1970 and 2000, lines that matched the MIT researcher's figures nearly exactly. Every line takes a dramatic nosedive between 2025 and 2050.

Like all the newly converted, I spent months in states of hypersensitivity to my new reality, a wild-eyed, skinless alertness, intense incredulity at the unbelief of others, a relentless impulse to evangelize, accompanied by a kind of paranoia (maybe not paranoia, after all) about a world that had conspired to withhold Big Truth from me. We didn't yet have the language of 'climate grief', and now that we do I don't know how helpful it is. It's only in a world-sense that imagines the earth and all of creation as separate from human kinship that *climate* grief becomes its own category. I knew somehow at the time that the deaths of friends and relationships and reckoning with queer identity and losing the earth were intertwining wildernesses, each grief deepening the others. Still, I held faithfully to one of the few assurances I have as a writer, that nearly every splintering of the self can, with time, be re-collected in language. This is no mere metaphor; neuroscience has shown that not only is the brain plastic, the hippocampus, which is responsible for memories, emotions and learning, regenerates quite rapidly. Moreover, the gut, sometimes referred to as the 'second brain', does as much (if not more) of what we imagine the brain does: thinks, feels, builds blocks of behaviours that turn into moods, convictions, identities. And those cells regenerate every two to nine days. We are made and remade, fearfully and wonderfully, and continually.

So, I had wanted to reframe loss – of family, of futures – by writing about the past, exploring Big Grief (having settled into it a little) through the apocalyptic texts I was studying in 2014, particularly the book of Fourth Ezra. Frighteningly specific numbers had started to appear in headlines: '12 years to act to avert climate disaster', or, '12 years? More like 18 months'. It seemed an opportune moment to write about apocalypses. Then in January of 2020 my 43-year-old brother died suddenly and inexplicably (non-drinking, non-smoking, fearful of recreational drugs) of a heart attack. Exorbitant funerary transport costs meant that he was cremated before friends or family, thousands of miles away, could see him. I flew to the USA, and three weeks after I returned to Ireland, where I live, the entire world constricted with the Covid-19 pandemic. 'I didn't get to say good-bye' ascended like a chorus of lament; my voice was just one of many. I'd like to tell you more about my brother, about the world that ended when he left the world, but that is for a different essay. More recently, another *Guardian* headline reads, 'World has 6 months to avert climate crisis, says energy expert'.

Here is where I find myself now: not only is apocalypse not a subject of the past, but much like grief, it does not conform to linear time or logical narrative at all. There is not a straightforward way forward. Wherever you are reading this, please do not forget that we are not in control, we do not know everything, and that our end – the end of all creatures – is still, always, continually unfolding.

In *The Apocalyptic Imagination*, John Collins describes apocalyptic writing as

> revelatory literature with a narrative framework, in which a revelation is mediated by an otherworldly being to a human recipient, disclosing a transcendent reality which is both temporal, insofar as it envisages eschatological salvation, and spatial insofar as it involves another, supernatural world.[2]

So, a story about divine revelation, through visions or otherworldly journeys, knowledge about end times, final judgement, and the establishing of God's kingdom. The apocryphal book of Fourth Ezra is an apocalypse partially composed sometime after the Romans destroyed Jerusalem in AD 70. The true author is unknown, but in the story the Jewish scribe Ezra, exiled in Babylon sometime between the sixth and fifth centuries BC, pleads with God to help him understand why God allows evil in God's own creation. In response Ezra receives seven visions through the mediation of the archangel Uriel. Again and again, Ezra demands quantitative, logical answers to many anxious, often angry, questions that I, as a dual US–EU citizen, can very much relate to:

Why is an evil empire allowed to continue to wreak havoc on those who honour their covenant with God?

When the angel responds that the current world will pass, Ezra's desperation deepens: *When will the new age come? How much time remains?* (12 years? 18 months? 6 months?)

When and how will the end come? (Plague? Wars? Collapse of biodiversity and food systems? Fires and floods? Acidification of the oceans? Arctic methane burps?)

Why do we have to wait and suffer through successive generations? Why did God not make all of creation at the same time and pass judgement immediately? (So why is God not more like Twitter?)

---

2 John J. Collins, 1998, *The Apocalyptic Imagination: An Introduction to Jewish Apocalyptic Literature*, Grand Rapids, MI: Eerdmans, p. 5.

Is there more time behind us or ahead of us? (The answer to this one seems obvious.)

Will there be more who are damned than saved? Will I be alive in those days? Why make the world only to destroy it?

I feel the question behind Ezra's question here: why make us as we are, and then destroy us for being as we are?

The angel's responses are, shall we say, less than consoling:

> Lo, the days are coming when those who inhabit the earth shall be seized with great terror, and the way of truth shall be hidden, and the land shall be barren of faith ... the land that you now see ruling shall be a trackless waste, and people shall see it desolate ... And one shall reign whom those who inhabit the earth do not expect, and the birds shall fly away together; and the Dead Sea shall cast up fish; and one whom the many do not know shall make his voice heard by night, and all shall hear his voice. There shall be chaos also in many places, fire shall often break out, the wild animals shall roam beyond their haunts. (Fourth Ezra 5.1, 3, 6–8).

It is easy to ascribe the power of this text to the way it seems to predict *this* moment of terror, fake news, confusion, collapse of ecosystems, fires, displaced wildlife. With a little reflection, the text feels like an oracle in nearly all of its details. I am reminded of the ways the black freedom movement in the USA was born under the precarious cover of 'hush harbors', as the religion of the enslaved; once heard only by night, now all hear the voice of the movement affirming that Black Lives Matter.[3] But that oracular quality is just one source of its power. Another is its formal disregard of linear time. This text, remember, was written after the destruction of Jerusalem in AD 70, as if written in the BC past by a Jewish prophet (Ezra) who is predicting the destruction of Jerusalem in the future.

---

3 See for example, the Revd Eboni Marshall Turman's article, 2020, 'A Theological Statement from the Black Church on Juneteenth', *Colorlines*, 19 June, www.colorlines.com/articles/theological-statement-black-church-juneteenth, accessed 30/06/20.

Why would such a genre exist? Much like authors of speculative and science fiction, the apocalyptic writers might have used time-bending narratives and revelation (rather than linear, rational arguments) as a strategy to hold the psyche intact, to imagine possibilities of life, and to create at least an illusion of control, during times of profound and widespread uncertainty, when logic and reason would predict only further ruin. For example, against the backdrop of settler-colonialist state destruction and denigration of black and indigenous life, Afrofuturist and indigenous futurist forms of art and literature affirm (among other things) that black and indigenous people exist and thrive in the future. It is a way of acknowledging, maybe as the apocalyptic writers of Fourth Ezra were doing, that, again, we are not in control, that we cannot know everything, and that there is power (even divine power) in the imagination.

And let's remember that, according to Collins' definition, apocalypses play with space as well as time, as we can see in one particularly pivotal vision: following Uriel's instructions, Ezra goes to 'a field of flowers where no house has been built, and eat[s] only of the flowers of the field' (Fourth Ezra 9.24, NRSV) for seven days. There he meets a woman weeping alone over the death of her son. Emboldened by his previous encounters with the angel, Ezra assumes an authoritative position and admonishes the woman harshly for her individual grief: 'You most foolish of women, do you not see our mourning, and what has happened to us? ... you are sorrowing for one son, but we, the whole world, for our mother' (Fourth Ezra 10.6, 8, NRSV). At the moment when he softens and expresses sincere empathy, she begins to transform physically. In Ezra's account:

Her face suddenly began to shine exceedingly; her countenance flashed like lightning, so that I was too frightened to approach her, and my heart was terrified. While I was wondering what this meant, she suddenly uttered a loud and fearful cry, so that the earth shook at the sound. When I looked up, the woman was no longer visible to me, but a city was being built, and a place of huge foundations showed itself. (Fourth Ezra 10.25–27, NRSV)

The woman, in fact, was the angel's allegorical figure for Zion, or the city of Jerusalem, rebuilt.

There are a few key moments in this text when Ezra is in the realm of certainties: first, in the beginning during his lengthy, historical, 'evidence-based' accusation of God, and here, when he is reproaching the weeping woman. In both cases, the source of his authority is primarily his own human intellect, specifically, his rational, linear argument; in both cases, revelation – the unveiling of all that he doesn't know – shatters his self-righteousness, making way for a more compassionate positioning within his own suffering. Later in the text, the angel commissions Ezra to write the story of the world, and, more importantly, instructs, 'set your house in order, and reprove your people; comfort the lowly among them, and instruct those that are wise' (Fourth Ezra 14.13, NRSV). The consolation is not a triumphant hope that disaster and suffering won't take place, but a call for Ezra first to mind himself and his own affairs, then meeting others where they are according to their capacity to receive, rather than engaging in blanket proselytizing about the end of the world. It would not be an exaggeration to say that in 2014 I was constitutionally changed by the deep wisdom of this moment in the text, which also helped me move from a position of (first grief-stricken, then self-righteous) alienation, towards a more participatory belonging in the world, even while acknowledging that the world I knew was, and is, dying.

I am not suggesting that scientific data collected and analysed over the last century (in fact, awareness of climate change predates the twentieth century) is wrong, nor am I suggesting that a biblical text necessarily provides answers that scientific research can't. I am looking, instead, with a degree of suspicion at the ways we cling to certainties in the Anthropocene. Even the idea of the Anthropocene, which emerged from a 'Western' intellectual tradition to name the age of calamitous human impact on the earth, relies on binaries (we can only 'save' or 'lose' the earth), data sets, doomsday clocks, evidence-based projections of the exact hour of our demise – habits of thinking similar to those that have led to the disaster. What if the truth is something more humble, and strange, and queer?

29

Ritualizing Grief

PANU PIHKALA

When I think of my climate grief, I see many shades of sorrow, but also a range of other emotions. Grief is a conglomerate, a matrix, a bundle of threads.

'The important point is not to achieve, but to strive,' wrote the pioneering conservationist Aldo Leopold more than 50 years ago.[1] In 2011, I ended my first theological text about climate change by quoting him. Back then, I was already grappling with the question of whether success was possible in climate politics, but my thinking and emotions were not as explicit as they would later become. When I look at my writings, speeches and journal entries from the early 2010s, I see more elegy than I feel now, even though my sense of totality of the ongoing catastrophe has grown. Unrecognized grief tends to increase elegy and melancholy. However, both then and now, I emphasized meaningfulness, and characterized hope mainly as meaning-making.

In a workshop in 2010, the springtime sun was shining brightly outside, but inside the people were nervous and silent. On the table was a black cloth, and on top of it was an animal skull, various pieces of trash collected from the surrounding environment, a Bible and a burning candle. In the midst of a two-day course for church workers – pastors, youth workers, deacons – about Christian ecotheology, we had organized a session where the focus was on dark ecological emotions. Essi Aarnio-Linnanvuori, an experienced environmental educator, was my partner in leading the course. Since there was usually never a

---

1 A. Leopold, 1993 [1955], *Round River: From the Journals of Aldo Leopold*, Oxford and New York: Oxford University Press.

chance for people to really focus on eco-anxiety, we wanted to provide a unique opportunity.

The group had already established a sense of communal security over the previous day. Prior to the session, we discussed ecological problems, and now we read laments from the Bible, giving participants time before the 'altar' and inviting them to write prayers on paper. Gradually the texts moved towards more hope, without losing the sense of tragedy. Finally, we moved outside into the open air and sunshine, and together planted a tree sapling. Church coffee followed a small open-air service. The people, who had been sorrowful and anxious, now smiled buoyantly and lively chatter filled the air.

This was the start of my work in organizing explicit sessions about dark ecological emotions. The feedback and evaluation of the aforementioned session showed it had worked: it had been poignant and relieving for the participants, despite the anxiety and intensity in the session. In psychological language, we had managed to hold and contain. But even before the session we realized that these kinds of activities require careful planning and caution. This is a tricky thing, because these activities are so new that one has to start despite incomplete knowledge. But there is a difference between recklessness and a recognized incompleteness.

The fate of a certain forest taught me a lot. In spring 2015, an ancient coniferous forest near to Hvitträsk, a famous mansion built by Eliel Saarinen and his colleagues, was suddenly clearcut by the government. The forest was already ancient when the architects built their home over a hundred years ago, and the pristine nature of the place was an important reason for their selection of this setting. Lots of spruce and pine trees, wide canopies of dark-green moss, and a steep descent into a clear blue lake. Eliel Saarinen and a few others were buried in the forest because of its beauty and significance. Since the mansion had been a state-owned museum for decades, both travellers and locals liked to spend time in this wood.

I read the news at home and was shocked. I had spent much time in this forest and knew about its significance both as an ecosystem and for people. I was on paternal leave with my two-year-old, so I packed him and my bike on to the local train and went to investigate. I am one of those relatively phlegmatic Nordic persons, shaped by the cold winters and safe childhood environments. But this time I truly felt moral outrage and eco-anger. Almost all the trees had been cut down. The heavy machines had ruined much of the blueberries. The devastation extended almost to the gravesite. The state officials tried to explain that the trees were dangerous for people, since they were so old, but this wasn't actually true; a biologist analysed the stumps and pointed out that only one or two were unhealthy. They had just wanted to cut down the forest, to make a bit of profit and to follow their standard procedures for forest 'management'.

The next day, I decided to organize a public lament for this woodland. The mere suggestion of a lament of this kind had a political dimension to it, since it is not customary in Finland – a country greatly dependent historically on forest industry – to publicly mourn trees, even ancient ones. But I did my best to focus on grief in the lament, since I firmly believe that grief rituals should be about expressing emotions, not places of agitation. The political message will carry itself through implicitly.

In a drizzle, 30 people showed up. The local church musician joined me and played cello from a van, to protect the instrument from rain. We constructed a rough altar of cut-down tree branches, which we set to a shape of a cross which leaned on a large tree stump. There were no official structures for such a ritual available, so I had to be creative. I used practically all the elements of a funeral ritual. The Bible lessons talked about trees and grief. Instead of throwing sand on a coffin, I touched the stump as a symbolic act of saying farewell and praying for transcendental life. In the case of the forest, life after death would follow in the form of new trees, but it would take decades.

People expressed their grief and paid their farewells to this much-loved wood. Some participated in singing and in touching the ground, some decided to stay still, and all reactions were explicitly allowed and endorsed. Catharsis happened, even though all righteous anger did not disappear. That wasn't the purpose, either. Afterwards, people spontaneously gathered on the yard of the mansion and started discussing future actions to prevent something like this from happening again. The main

Christian magazine in Finland ran a story about the lament and information about it spread.

Hvitträsk forest taught me many things. First, that anger and outrage can motivate action. Second, that it is possible to organize public rituals for ecological grief. I could apply my experience and skills as a pastor to ecology-related rituals. I found the work of Joanna Macy, which provided more education on these matters, as did theologian Steven Chase's work.[2] Macy's four-phase model of encountering difficult emotions starts from acknowledging gratitude, which I started to include more explicitly in my workshops; in Macy and Brown's book *Coming Back to Life*, there was a vast array of rituals, activities and practical tips, including weeping practices.[3] Chase applied old Christian contemplative spirituality to various emotions related to nature, which gave further ideas. He even gave instructions for writing laments related to ecological damage and extinctions.

Later, I adapted this experience to the work of organizing rituals related to climate grief. That is more difficult, since climate grief is, currently, mostly transitional grief and anticipatory mourning. It is easier to mourn and to organize rituals if there is a specific subject, either a body of a creature or a lost place. But various kinds of rituals, or ritual-like events, related to climate grief have still been possible, and they have helped many people. We humans are bodily creatures, even though in Christianity we've often forgotten that. Being present with other bodies, or bodyminds, affects us holistically. Sometimes the body helps the mind. In grief rituals, it is very important that people can move their bodies in the ways that they feel suitable.

I read more about theories of grief and grieving practices. I lifted up the idea that acute climate-related loss could be encountered by rituals, if there were people who had prepared for that. Later these kinds of rituals were organized for the grief that people had because of the forest fires in Australia and Amazon.

---

2 S. Chase, 2011, *Nature as Spiritual Practice*, Grand Rapids, MI: Eerdmans.

3 J. Macy and M. Brown, 2014, *Coming Back to Life: The Updated Guide to the Work that Reconnects*, rev. edn, Gabriola Island, BC: New Society Publishers.

For transitional and anticipatory grief, I wondered about the possibilities of adapting some of the seasons and days from the Church year. Why not days and seasons for climate grief? Or for climate-related gratitude? I've been musing about Autumn Equinox as a theme day for ecological grief and climate grief. The symbolic and physical aspects of that season would support the content, and it would fit inside the 'Season of Creation' theme weeks that many congregations follow.

The work of North American writer and activist Trebbe Johnson provided further ideas and support.[4] She advocates for encountering wounded places and giving space for the development of spontaneous 'guerrilla beauty', perhaps, say, in the form of a bird constructed from natural materials amid a devastated place. Rituals need thresholds and it's useful if these are physical, not just spoken instructions of setting aside a time; that's why various churches and temples have special entrances, such as portals or gates. Johnson recommends setting these for rituals of ecological grief. Even a branch, which is set as a threshold, can function as a transitional element. These kinds of symbolic elements can be used also in city surroundings, for example by setting a colourful band of cloth as a threshold into a ritual space on a city square. The books by grief specialist Francis Weller provided further ideas and encouraged even more ritual imagination.[5]

I noticed that in addition to specific rituals, there can be permanent memorial places which help people to encounter their ecological grief and climate grief. The Monument to Passenger Pigeon in the USA is one example, and the Mass Extinction Memorial Observatory in Britain is another. On a local level, there can be set aside places for climate grief. Regarding symbolic architecture or design, there are several options here, but I've found elements of transitiveness important: perhaps near a sea or river shore, or next to a place which is changing because of climate breakdown. Even buildings or industrial areas can func-

---

4 T. Johnson, 2018, *Radical Joy for Hard Times: Finding Meaning and Making Beauty in Earth's Broken Places*, Berkeley, CA: North Atlantic Books.

5 F. Weller, 2015, *The Wild Edge of Sorrow: Rituals of Renewal and the Sacred Work of Grief*, Berkeley, CA: North Atlantic Books.

tion as such symbolic settings. The emotion of solastalgia (Glenn Albrecht's neologism: desire for solace + nostalgia + desolation[6]) – homesickness even though you are still living at home – can be addressed by such places.

My second book about eco-anxiety focused on the wide scale of various ecological emotions.[7] There's several of them that need rituals or public acknowledgements, and many of them can be linked with grief processes. Despair is one, anger is another. In some climate-related rituals, public acts or 'performances' focus on ways to channel anger constructively. This often happens in climate demonstrations: people can use their anger for embodied action, in a non-violent way. The fact that this is done together strengthens the impact, but the downside is that these events can further intensify the lines between 'us' and 'them'. Sometimes both grief and anger can be processed in a single event, but this requires careful preparation.

Questions related to despair and hope are nearly always present in endeavours related to the ecological crisis. My strategy has been to advocate a 'tragic hope'.[8] I do not lie when somebody asks whether I am optimistic about the future. But I do not endorse collapse language either, because its psycho-spiritual consequences are difficult to tell. Many people are already despairing enough. I believe that the way forward is from genuine emotional support and further recognition of dark ecological emotions, so that we can build resilience. My own climate grief is in a kind of acceptance stage. There is joy in life, even in the midst of these very difficult global ecological circumstances. A deep sadness about the future persists, but it does not command the whole of life. There is still deep meaning in this pilgrimage.

---

6 G. Albrecht, 2019, *Earth Emotions: New Words for a New World*, Ithaca, NY: Cornell University Press.

7 P. Pihkala, 2019, *Mieli maassa? Ympäristötunteet* (Ecological Emotions), Helsinki: Kirjapaja.

8 P. Pihkala, 2018, 'Eco-anxiety, Tragedy, and Hope: Psychological and Spiritual Dimensions of Climate Change, *Zygon* 53(2), pp. 545–69; P. Pihkala, 2017, 'Environmental Education after Sustainability: Hope in the Midst of Tragedy, *Global Discourse* 7(1), pp. 109–27.

30

The Earth is the Lord's: Finding a Way to Worship in Times of Despair

MAGGI DAWN

Between 2014 and 2019 I was invited to lead worship at a series of conferences organized to explore theological responses to ecological issues. These gatherings were broadly similar to most academic conferences, alternating between keynote speakers, short papers and break-out discussions, but in addition a short service of gathered worship was offered at the beginning and end of each day, and a lengthy service of worship to close each conference.

The majority of presentations and debates had a sobering, if not despairing tone, and the organizers, attuned to the fact that lament is somewhat under-utilized within the Christian tradition, had initially imagined worship that would take on the tone of a funeral or memorial for the earth. I was therefore asked to create a series of laments for the earth, rather than celebrations of faith. While lament was, at least in part, an appropriate response, I found myself questioning the wisdom of creating worship that seemed to express unmitigated despair with no future hope. The Psalmists, whose songs of celebration and lament the Christian tradition inherited from the Hebrew Bible, hold back nothing in terms of expressing their raw, heartfelt expressions of grief, yet in the context of their cries for help lie several accompanying ideas, each of which is present within Christian theology. The first, located in the lament psalms themselves, is the recurring theme that even in the darkest times, and even when the future seems unimaginable, there is still reason to hope. The second is a recognition of the trajectory of movement in Christian theology that redemption never looks backwards, always forwards. And the third – a theme that St Paul later develops enticingly – was the idea that our redemption is envisioned not from the earth but with it. As I began to plan for the worship, then, I began to weave these ideas together.

Hope in despair

The psalms of lament offer a structure both for personal prayer and gathered worship in times of grief or distress. While just one solitary psalm lands with absolutely no note of relief or hope for the future, most have a structure that breaks down into five stages. It is noticeable that the lament psalms often begin with an affirmation of God's presence. One of the most common human responses to tragedy is a sensation of abandonment – 'My God, my God, why have you forsaken me?' 'Where was God when ...?' – yet, despite these familiar feelings of anger and heartbreak, the Psalmists routinely begin by stating that, no matter how we feel, God is still with us. Second, having affirmed God's presence, they give full vent to their woes, naming what has caused their pain, but usually without any request beyond a cry for help. A further affirmation of God's presence follows, often with a reminder that God never failed in times gone by. 'I will call to mind the deeds of the LORD,' says a psalm of Asaph, 'I will remember your wonders of old' (Psalm 77.11, NRSV). The fourth stage in the lament is a reiteration of the predicament, this time in more detail, and with prayers of petition, asking God for solutions – sustenance in physical or mental illness, rescue from danger, defence against enemies, or whatever the situation demands. The fifth stage is a final proclamation of faith that God will help in the future. This pattern is not uniform throughout, but it does appear repeatedly – and, with the one exception of Psalm 88, the laments do all resolve into hope, not glib statements that everything will be all right, but a stubborn, defiant faith that, against the odds, and even despite my better judgement, 'I believe that I shall see the goodness of the LORD in the land of the living' (Psalm 27.13, NRSV). Despite the gnawing fear that God has abandoned us, or even worse is not there at all, the pattern of lament revolves around a stubborn insistence that God is, in fact, present even in disaster. Anchoring hope between the recollection of God's faithfulness in the past and promises for the future creates a canopy or web across the fear of abandonment in the present. The profound truth that emerges from this is that hope, which neither denies the bleakness of present reality nor demands immediate answers, is not invested in believable outcomes, prescient knowledge or practical solutions, but in the person of God. I have used this psalm structure many times to build liturgies of lament in response to both local and national tragedies. In the context of contemplating ecological disaster, again it offered a way to worship that enabled the expression of sorrow and despair, while grounding lament in a God of hope.

Forwards, not backwards

As the conference series began to unfold, it seemed that the raw facts about the ecological crisis tended to unanchor the theological response. This is not only unsurprising but entirely appropriate; throughout the history of Christian theology, its doctrines have always been subject to re-examination and interpretation at moments when global events have led to dramatic shifts in culture and ideas.[1] Game-changing developments in scientific enquiry (which are, arguably, less a reaction against Christian belief than a direct result of it) that initially seemed to challenge doctrine have ultimately precipitated its re-evaluation and reframing. The current ecological crisis is just such a moment. The message had shifted from one of an urgency to halt the decline to a more sobering acknowledgement of irreparable damage, and this created a crisis for theological response. For, how can future hope

1 See more in Maggi Dawn, 2017, 'The Deluge and a New Theology of Suffering', in Ayla Lepine (ed.), In Focus: The Deluge 1920 by Winifred Knights, Tate Research Publication, www.tate.org.uk/research/publications/in-focus/the-deluge/new-theology-of-suffering, accessed 04.06.2020.

be reaffirmed against a narrative that suggests there may be no future at all, at least for the earth? Questions of this magnitude, in addition to challenging the rational aspects of theological thinking, provoke an emotional response – and this began to emerge as the undercurrent to the gatherings. Between lectures and papers, over their 'paleo' lunches, people talked wistfully of the garden of Eden, embodying a mixture of regret for what was genuinely lost and nostalgia for an imagined past. There was a keen awareness that the clock could not be turned back, historically or scientifically, but the theological conversation remained lodged in the idea of a lost paradise. What was getting lost in those conversations was that the Christian theological vision, rather than looking back to the garden, moves forwards to the New Jerusalem, a garden city in which the built environment is in perfect harmony with the natural world. Christian theology has always insisted that our lives extend beyond the grave, and that something of our earthly existence is preserved and remade within that vision. To me, the idea of creating worship as a kind of funeral for the earth seemed out of kilter with this. To reiterate the Psalmist's heartfelt cry for help in desperate circumstances was exactly the right response, but to build worship around a theological narrative that mourns an unrecoverable past, and writes off the future as hopeless, is not only emotionally draining but also incongruous with a theology that looks forward to a future yet unwritten, in which we have an active part to play.

Redemption – with, not from, the earth

Looking forward does not necessarily mean that the slate is wiped clean and everything starts again. Framing the future in dualistic language is misleading, both for salvation and for eschatology, if it implies that the soul is saved apart from the body, or that a 'heavenly' future is entirely separable from earthly existence. Christian theology is more subtle, and more exciting, than that; salvation is envisaged not merely as a restoration of what was lost, but a re-creation that incorporates, rather than replaces, what already exists. The result is something better than before: resurrection is more than mere resuscitation. As for what 'heaven' means, it is a fool's errand to attempt any concrete detail. Nevertheless, woven through the eschatological vision in the New Testament there is, alongside the idea that our present reality will pass away, another thread suggesting that whatever 'heaven' might mean, it may not be unrelated to our present physical reality. Bodies, earth, trees, rivers, leaves – all these and more are envisaged as being remade in the heavenly vision, rather than discarded in favour of something entirely new. The paradox between the idea of something entirely new and something remade reverberates throughout Christian theology. In the current vernacular, you could perhaps compare this to the practice of 'upcycling' – a piece remade out of something old and broken is seen as more valuable than something completely new, its beauty and value being derived both from the salvage and preservation of its history and the artistry invested in its newly imagined state.

Heaven has not, of course, always been framed in this way, and the emphasis on leaving this world behind entirely has sometimes overshadowed the idea of re-creation. Especially during oppression or pain, the promise of heaven has acted as a panacea to sustain people through inescapable misery. But while one would never deny hope to those in the most extreme circumstances, the idea of heaven as entirely new and separate from this life can also function as escapism, with the undesired consequence of removing any incentive to struggle against the inequities or injustice that produce the suffering. Robert Beckford has written eloquently about how, in the context of racial injustice, a community can effectively be disempowered if its people find too much solace in the promise of heaven, and rather than marshalling anger to right the situation they can accidentally end up colluding with the very system that visits injustice on them.[2] The dynamic he describes is mirrored in theological responses that fail to engage with the urgency of ecological injustice by seeking too much comfort in the idea that there is a better world to come, and that we will eventually leave this earth behind.

2 Robert Beckford, 2001, *God of the Rahtid: Redeeming Rage*, London: Darton, Longman and Todd.

The New Testament writings suggest a more subtle relationship between earth and heaven, and between our redemption and
that of the earth. St Paul famously wrote that creation waits on
tiptoe – on tenterhooks – to see us redeemed. But he follows that
idea with this: 'Creation itself will be liberated from its bondage
to decay and brought into the freedom and glory of the children
of God' (Romans 8.21, NIV). Creation, according to Paul, is not
waiting for us to be liberated *from* the earth, but for the whole
created order – us and the earth – to be liberated together. The
biblical narratives open plenty of windows on to the idea that we
belong within creation, rather than it merely being a backdrop to
the human drama. Moses, for instance, took off his shoes as he
stood on holy ground; his transformative experience of holiness
occurred not by his being lifted off the ground, but by feeling
his connection to it; revelation and divine encounter regularly
occur not by abandoning the earth but by identifying particular
places, such as mountain tops, that serve as a liminal space where
two worlds collide. While gnostic or dualistic spiritualities separate the body from the soul, and colonial thinking begins from
the presumption that the earth is to be owned and subdued, the
biblical narratives seem rather to reinforce the idea that our
identity and our salvation are inseparable from the stuff of our
bodies, and our place on the earth.

With all of this in mind, I attempted to create space for worship
that wove these ideas together: that salvation is of the whole
person, not only the soul; that our redemption is tied up with
that of the earth; that a Christian theological response to the
earth's distress needs to look not backwards but forwards, to a
yet unimagined future, and in framing cries of lament we never
do so without hope. It was not difficult to combine prayers, readings, sounds and silence to give expression to these, but there
were very few hymns and songs that seemed to meet the occa-
sion. Many traditional hymns celebrate the glories of creation,
but they portray everything from mountains to forests to rivers
and birds singing in the trees in a romantically untroubled landscape; nowhere is there a polluted river or a dangerously red
sky. Stirring though these hymns are, they would have sounded
hollow at a conference on ecological disaster. I needed songs

that affirmed the created order as God's gift (Psalm 24.1) while also acknowledging the distress of the earth; songs that would neither deny the current predicament nor resolve into despair. This, then, was the backdrop for this new song that at one and the same time gives thanks for the earth, laments its woes and expresses hope and longing for a promised future in which we, and the land we belong to, might see salvation:

> The earth is the Lord's, and everything in it,
> From seabed to sky, and from ocean to earth,
> The beauty from here to the farthest horizon –
> A gift to us all from the moment of birth.
>
> Can you feel the aching heart of creation? –
> A planet in peril, a world in despair,
> A habitat drained of strength and resilience
> Can never sustain all the life in her care.
>
> *There is no way back to the Garden of Eden,*
> *But the vision you promise is a city and home,*
> *Redeem us, O Lord, and the land we belong to,*
> *Creation still groans for a new world to come.*
>
> On this holy ground, defenceless before you,
> Your Spirit, O God, is the air that we breathe,
> O teach us to live your holy vocation
> To care for the ground that is under our feet.
>
> *There is no way back to the Garden of Eden,*
> *but the vision you promise is a city and home,*
> *Redeem us, O Lord, and the land we belong to,*
> *Creation still groans for a new world to come.*
> (© 2017 Maggi Dawn)

31

The Wrath of God

ARCHUNA ANANTHAMOHAN

I write this in the midst of a global pandemic. And as billions stay at home, fearing for their lives and futures, this historic crisis has compelled many of us to wake up. We've realized that life on this planet is precious and is something too many of us take for granted. We've learnt that nothing is politically 'impossible' to achieve. That it's perfectly possible to tackle homelessness, alleviate poverty and stand by the most vulnerable.

This pandemic has shown that if one of us suffers, we all do. And that the only way we can survive this is to love one another. Individuals, communities, governments and organizations are all playing a key part in surviving this pandemic. Clearly, showing compassion for all of God's creation is not just an individual task but a systemic one too. And it is that love for all of God's creation that sustains me during these challenging times.

It is horrifying, therefore, to see fear and hatred being used to justify this crisis: 'It's a punishment from God!'; 'We are the virus!'; 'The most vulnerable were a burden anyway'. As the pandemic is intrinsically connected to the environment, it shouldn't surprise us that there have been similar remarks made about the climate crisis.

Earlier last year, I was observing the Extinction Rebellion protests in London. There was an iconic moment when a barricade of climate activists blocked a small road, holding placards about the climate crisis. A doomsday preacher suddenly appeared, waving his hand, dismissing the protesters as he cackled, 'God doesn't care about the environment! God cares about your souls!'

My family are from Sri Lanka. It is an island renowned for its natural beauty and local hospitality. But this beautiful island also has a darker history of war, ethnic cleansing and pogroms. For decades, the country's minority Tamil population were persecuted by successive governments. In the final civil war, up to 70,000 Tamil civilians in the Tamil-dominated north were believed to have been massacred. War crimes have been brushed aside as many of those responsible today enjoy political immunity.

Today, we hear terrifying reports of military occupation and oppression of the Tamil-dominated north. Already impoverished, many are now dying due to increasing levels of drought and famine. Recently, the Global Climate Risk Index ranked Sri Lanka as the second-most-impacted country from climate change. Northern-occupied areas were assessed as the worst affected, demonstrating how climate change contributes to ongoing political oppression. Indeed, throughout the island, the climate emergency has disrupted thousands of people's livelihoods, many of whom depend on the agricultural economy.

I have many water-coloured memories of the paradise that is Sri Lanka. From competing with mischievous monkeys to marvelling at the magnificent hills, God's creation filled me with such awe and wonder as a child. I now lament her death and worry about what is to come. As the climate crisis disproportionately affects the economic stability of developing nations like Sri Lanka, many islanders will desperately demand political stability. This, as we've seen in recent times, often appeals to the nation's ethnonationalist and fascist tendencies. And it will be the country's Christian, Muslim and Tamil minority populations that will continue to suffer as a result.

So what next for all my friends and loved ones back in Sri Lanka? Will they survive the floods and cyclones? Will our homes be safe from both climate and political activity? What will become of this green and pleasant land?

As I mourn the loss of our wildlife, I mourn the loss of a people too. Indeed, my own sense of belonging may soon be lost. In the West, eco-fascist sentiments are being normalized. Instead of tackling unjust and unsustainable systems that prioritize fossil fuel consumption and profit, 'overpopulation' has become the easy scapegoat for why this crisis is happening. Talk of 'overpopulation' and 'mass migration' is legitimizing a media narrative that darker-skinned foreigners are the problem. Tamil refugees continue to be deported by the British government, only to be tortured and killed once they've left. And with climate change now being used to justify highly anti-immigrant and racist 'hostile environment' policy-making, I fear what this might one day entail for families like mine.

So when I hear preachers make tone-deaf remarks about God not caring about the environment or that the devastating loss of human life is somehow a punishment from God, I'm furious. I hear the infuriating implication that God doesn't care about God's own creation and that the lives of the poorest and most vulnerable people were always expendable in the eyes of God. Such a callous disregard for life is deeply contrary to the Way of Christ. So how do we make sense of God's 'wrath' in this time of grief? Defining wrath as God's vengeful retribution does little to heal a sick world.

In *Stages of Faith*, theologian James W. Fowler classifies spiritual development in terms of stages.[1] At each stage, one's spiritual understanding is said to deepen, as is the capacity to love. This is something observed by mystics across many faith traditions, most notably in the Sufi Islamic tradition. In Fowler's classification, Stage Two of spiritual development describes a 'mythic-literal' understanding of faith. At such a level, the individual's understanding of justice and morality is based on reward and punishment. Meanwhile, metaphors and symbolic language are frequently mistaken to be literal. While stages often correlate with people's ages, it is clear that many people have not passed Stage-Two thinking.

There are countless passages in Hebrew and New Testament Scriptures that have been understood in Stage-Two framing. These passages are often understood to portray God's 'wrath' as an eternal punishment in a literal hell. This does not mean that these passages were originally understood with a Stage-Two insight, however. Bradley Jersak beautifully conveys this

---

1 James W. Fowler, 1981, *Stages of Faith: The Psychology of Human Development and the Quest for Meaning*, New York: HarperCollins.

in *A More Christlike God*,[2] where he encourages us to see how, throughout Scripture, 'wrath' can be understood very differently. Rather than literally interpreting 'wrath' as anger or vengeful retribution, we should instead see wrath as 'divine consent'.

God consents to our freedom. By allowing us to act however we want, we inevitably make mistakes and fall short of the glory of God (Romans 3.23). However, sin is not only defined in terms of individual shortcomings but systemic ones too. We only need to think of how the prophets of the Hebrew Bible would mightily denounce the unfaithfulness of entire nations and domination systems to recognize the systemic nature of sin. In Sri Lanka, imperialism perpetuates such ecological and socio-economic injustice. The Chinese and Sri Lankan regimes have made lucrative deals to expand unsustainable development on the island. Such projects have served only the wealthiest and most corrupt, while violating international environmental standards. This has fuelled the decimation of fishing stock and the erosion of labour rights. In return for the exploitation of Sri Lankan land, we are seeing the Chinese government use its political power to prevent an international investigation into the alleged war crimes and human rights abuses committed by the Sri Lankan political class.

As we continue to worship the powerful fossil fuel industry as our idol, our planet continues to die and we all continue to suffer. When 'wrath' is thus framed as divine consent, we see how we are being punished *by* our sins, rather than *for* our sins. Sin carries its own penalty (Romans 6.23). Its harmful consequences reverberate across the universe. Thus, it is not God who is actively punishing us for our sins but ourselves.

This raises another question: does God's 'divine consent' mean that God is indifferent? While wrath may be divine consent, Jesus reminds us that we are not alone. Christ's death and resurrection is a declaration of the triumph of grace-infused solidarity – God's solidarity with us in the person of Jesus. When we find ourselves suffering due to man-made or natural events, we can derive strength from this cosmic act of solidarity. As a Tamil who grieves both the loss of his own people and the destruction

---

2 Bradley Jersak, 2015, *A More Christlike God: A More Beautiful Gospel*, Pasadena, CA: Plain Truth Ministries.

of God's sacred land, it is liberating to know that God suffers with you.

But understanding 'wrath' as 'divine consent' also demands us to act now. If it is not God who punishes us with the climate crisis but ourselves, we must all surely do better. We must channel these feelings of grief – of anger, loss and betrayal – into prophetic activism. What often stops people from getting more involved in climate activism is the recognition of the inescapability of complicity in our system. Yet, God's grace reminds us that we aren't perfect. Instead of worrying over unrealistic standards of purity and perfection, let us walk in love.

Jesus says, 'If anyone would come after me, let him deny himself and take up his cross and follow me' (Matthew 16.24, ESV). We are called to die to our old ways and bravely take up our crosses in solidarity. Let us no longer follow the imperial ways of ecocide and instead stand up for all of God's creation. For my family in Sri Lanka, this is a very empowering message. Our loss was never a punishment from God. Nor was our grief insignificant. 'Wrath' as divine cruciform consent reminds us that God is with us as we grieve. Christ is present in every act of radical, selfless love. If 'God is love', then the sins of this world will be overcome by divine Love. And as we become absorbed in eternal Love, we gain the clarity and strength to take up our crosses and live to fight another day.

32

Faithful, Not Successful

HOLLY-ANNA PETERSON

The crunch

He looked at his watch and with a muffled, 'That's all for today, everyone, thank you very much', the students around me started packing their books into their bags and leaving the lecture theatre. I lingered behind as they shuffled down the benches and out the door – aware that my body was becoming palpably hot and that I was struggling to take in breaths. I composed myself, focused on putting one foot in front of the other, and made my way out of the building, keeping my head down.

That was the first of a series of university lectures I had on how the climate crisis was affecting our planet – the changes to our biosphere, our ecosystems and the human suffering being inflicted. I sat through lecture after lecture of harrowing information – truths I not only had to absorb but go away and research further. I remember the sick feeling in my stomach when I learnt that the extinction rate was 1,000 times higher than it should be. I remember the shame I felt hearing of people being born into, living through and dying from malnutrition. I remember trying to comprehend global tipping points – that greenhouse gas emissions are reaching a point of no return, where our world is locked into feedback loops of perpetual heating.

I was 20 years old, but I was in a state of panicked disbelief at the world – trying to grapple with how people were going politely about their day when the backdrop was that the safety of our planetary home was being undone. I felt paralysed. On the one hand, I had a sense of profound urgency, caught in racing thoughts of quitting my degree to help tackle the crisis. But at the same time, I felt powerless to act. I was coming up short on what exactly tackling the crisis required of me and doubted I was brave enough to do what was needed.

The rejection

They stopped the video in a state of glee and scrolled down to show some of the other YouTube videos our church youth leader had created – 'eating a live goldfish', 'eating a live tarantula', 'drinking ten blended mice'. I was caught in a silence of disgust and horror as the room erupted with excited laughter around me. 'Isn't it hilarious? The RSPCA are trying to stop him but he's getting hundreds of thousands of views.'

At this time I was a relatively new Christian. I was still looking to others for what it meant to be part of this tribe. I soon came to learn that pretty much all members of my church held strong anthropocentric beliefs. As I began to express my eco-anxiety, my concern about animal suffering or ecological breakdown, it was quickly rebutted as an attack on God's love for humankind and branded un-Christian. This was a painful picture of faith: first there are humans – so focused on themselves that they erode the very earth they need to survive. Then there is a cold, uncaring creator that rejects the creation he fathomed into being.

Grappling with this is the closest I have come to leaving the Church. I did not want to be loved by a God that would set such a cosmos in motion, and I did not want to be part of a faith that was giving moral licence to destructive human behaviour. But after I had finished shouting out all my anger at God, I experienced comfort. Maybe, underneath all my frustration, the truth was that the God I was shouting at was actually grieving alongside me, mourning for our collective loss.

The paralysis

It's ten years later. I could hear her voice starting to break. 'It makes me ... so scared thinking of what's happening to the world with climate change.' She gulped down her anguish and I gave her some space to give her emotion words. 'What are things going to be like when my children get older?'

As an NHS mental health practitioner I have had multiple conversations like this one. More people are experiencing a deep sense of distress about the climate emergency we face. My experience from talking these things through is that when people realize the reality of the climate crisis, they can feel emotionally overwhelmed by anxiety or a sense of hopelessness. These feelings are difficult in themselves, but they are often exacerbated by the sting of guilt – that it's our lifestyles that have caused this destruction and our inaction that has allowed it to perpetuate. I remember how strong this feeling was for me. I would lie awake at night ruminating on how every day I chose not to step up; I was pushing more burden on to children and the poorest communities around the world who get hit the hardest by climate breakdown. I would feel the comfort of my bed knowing that in communities on the front line people are losing their lives trying to protect the environment they need to sustain themselves.

This heightened distress often leads to a sense of paralysis – we feel compelled to take the radical action needed to relieve our discomfort, but the prospect of putting this into practice can also feel very unsettling. In order to bring a sense of relief, we can be tempted to downplay the enormity of the climate crisis or avoid thinking about it. Obviously we can't spend our whole time dwelling on the crisis or we would be exhausted wrecks. However, if we turn to denial too often, we can get stuck in a spiral of inaction, guilt and distress – a pattern that is no longer helpful for us or our planet.

The call

The eventual balance, where we are able to sit with the reality of what is happening in our world and begin to take practical steps forward, is not an easy one to find. Outside of my day job I am one of the coordinators of a group called Christian Climate Action, which is the name given to the Christians of Extinction Rebellion. One of the phrases that we often remind on another of is 'we are called to be faithful, not successful' – a phrase spoken by prominent Christian figures of the past such as Mother Teresa. This has become a spiritual mantra to me, which has helped to create a positive cycle of increased action, motivation and comfort.

It may only be eight words, but they pack a lot of punch. Dorothy Day, the co-founder of the Catholic Worker Movement, discusses this theme in one of her letters:

> I don't expect any success in anything we are trying to do … But that the struggle will go on to such an extent that God will not let it hinder the work but that the work will go on, because that work is our suffering and our sanctification. So rejoice in failures, rejoice in suffering![1]

These powerful words show how taking this approach can ease an emotional grip by reminding us of our place as followers. Climate anxiety can become overwhelming when we feel as though the oncoming catastrophe is out of our control or too big for us to deal with. A call to be faithful urges us to relinquish our addiction to control and hand that over to God. It helps me not to focus on the overwhelming challenge of what 'success' would look like in this crisis, and instead to put my energy into the more manageable task of focusing on the here and now and answering the question, 'What does being faithful look like for me today?'

These words are not just helpful in soothing our distress for its own sake. The call to be faithful is a practical one. However,

---

1 Dorothy Day, 2012, *All the Way to Heaven: The Selected Letters of Dorothy Day*, ed. Robert Ellsberg, Milwaukee, WI: Marquette University Press, pp. 212–13.

an important feature of being faithful is that it is centred on relationship. It is so much more than 'doing the right thing' – instead,
we are encouraged faithfully to follow Christ. This relationship
is core to pulling us out of emotional paralysis. Instead of feeling
overwhelmed by the actions we need to make, we are drawn out
of our comfort zone by a love that 'casts out fear'. This relationship with our Christ also washes us with grace and forgiveness
– relieving the sting of guilt and allowing us to take each step
forward with humble repentance. The positive spiral that this
dynamic creates is often expressed by those on the ground at
climate protests, with many describing a cathartic joy amid the
stress and sacrifice. This experience is more than just a hope that
our action might create the change needed, it is an outpouring of
spiritual relationship.

A common misconception with the phrase 'we are called to
be faithful, not successful' is that we are aiming low – encouraging people to offer up token gestures, instead of meaningful
action that might make a real difference. However, we need to be
reminded of who we are invited to be faithful to. Our carpenter
Christ did not shy away from taking radical, sacrificial action. He
chose to take on the vulnerable form of flesh, to live among the
needy and to stand up for justice, despite knowing it would end
in a brutal, humiliating and excruciating execution. And he did
this even though he was afraid. Luke's Gospel tells us of Jesus,
in the garden of Gethsemane, that 'being in anguish, he prayed
more earnestly, and his sweat was like drops of blood falling to
the ground' (Luke 22.44, NIV). The challenge of being faithful
to such a Christ is to experience the hurricane of fear, grief and
hopelessness and answer the call for relationship anyway.

In my 9 to 5, I leave many of my identities at the door. I am
not a Christian, I am not an activist and I put aside my sociopolitical views. Instead of being concerned with justice, I focus
on empathy. Instead of looking at what is right and wrong, I
am looking for what is helpful. It's only when I get home and
step out of the practitioner persona that these testimonies join
together with others to make a larger picture of injustice. This
isn't just a random assortment of policy mistakes resulting in a
few unfortunate consequences. Those in positions of power are

inflicting intentional mass suffering. Reflecting on people's testimonies feels like listening to a collective cry. I feel as if I have dipped my toe into the well of human suffering. I wonder if this is a tiny insight into what God experiences – hearing the collective anguish of his creation 'as in the pains of childbirth'; the weeping and wailing around the world that seeps out of systematic sin. What would happen if we woke up tomorrow with the call to faithfulness ringing in our ears? Maybe we could channel our collective cry into a collective roar. The ferocious body of Christ, pushing against the odds, for earth as it is in heaven.

33

Becoming Grievable in Appalachia: Climate Trauma and Palliative Care

DEBRA MURPHY

The apprehension of another's precarity is implicitly an apprehension of our own. (Judith Butler)[1]

Introduction

For more than a hundred years, extractive industries have had their way with us in southern Appalachia. The assaults on land and water, bodies and spirits have been constant, calculated and often executed with astonishing stealth. The tactics of abuse – the sweet-talking, the gaslighting – are familiar to those who know how predators operate. Some victims have colluded with the perpetrators, claiming consent and, in a weird Stockholm Syndrome kind of way, asking for more. Others – individuals and whole communities – have tried to fight off the attackers, asserting their own dignity and that of the violated earth. Many have also longed for the plight of this place to be made visible beyond its borders, not in the cause of pity (God knows we are bored of people feeling sorry for us), but that our precarity – how

---

1 Throughout this essay I will draw on Judith Butler's treatment of precariousness, precarity and grievability in her books *Frames of War: When is Life Grievable?* (London: Verso, 2009) and *Precarious Life: The Power of Mourning and Violence* (London: Verso, 2006). This quote appears on p. xvi in *Frames of War*. I will also draw on my 2019 essay, 'Reading Genesis in a Dying World', *The Christian Century* 136(22), 23 October, p. 35.

our lives are always in some sense in the hands of others – would be recognized as a universally shared condition.[2]

Climate trauma in this precarious place, as in every place, leaves a trail of grief and broken-heartedness in its wake. It presents both the challenge and the gift of turning private pain into collective mourning. The death and dying around us now and yet to come make despair tempting. But acknowledging the loss of what we love witnesses to another gift: our belonging to one another and to all of creation. Bearing witness to this belonging, this deep connection, can take various forms. In the Christian tradition, there is a long history of keeping vigil over the dying, of not allowing them to be alone in their final days and hours. In such watchful waiting, we both grieve and hope. Palliative care is a set of practices on a continuum with hopeful vigilance, one that deepens our connection with the dying and can help to make sacred our sorrow and pain. In this essay, I suggest that it also offers a helpful analogy for the grief work necessary to rediscover belonging, hope and beauty in a dying world.

'The poor you will always have with you …'

Part of what prevents a meaningful response to the crisis of climate collapse is the disconnect most of us experience between fact and feeling. Knowing that something profound is true – a loved one has just died, the world as we know it is ending – and reckoning with that truth are processes that do not, and probably cannot, occur at the same time. Indeed, the more traumatic the 'fact', the more we tend affectively to dissociate from it. This can make grieving difficult since grief resides in the body – since grief is *felt* and not registered primarily in the intellect.

But what makes something or someone grievable? What status must be afforded a place or a people for their loss to elicit body-

2 Butler defines 'precariousness' as a feature of existence for all: there is no life without the need for shelter and food; no life that transcends injurability and mortality. 'Precarity' is a politically induced condition in which certain populations suffer from failing social and economic support systems and become differentially exposed to injury, violence and death. *Frames of War*, pp. 24–5.

felt grief? What frames or purposeful ways of seeing are in play when we recognize – or not – another's intrinsic dignity and likeness to ourselves? If we are unable to recognize that our lives and destinies are bound up with others in mutual precarity, then such places and people exist with 'no regard, no testimony, and [are] ungrieved when lost'.[3]

One of the frames through which Appalachia is routinely viewed is poverty. From the early 1960s, with the Johnson administration's 'war on poverty', to the 2016 presidential election and the pundit class's assumption that Appalachia is 'Trump Country', this geographically and culturally diverse region has been considered ground zero for America's disaffected, rural poor. It is also associated with a stable of longstanding literary and visual tropes like bare feet and backwardness, making it easy subject matter for poverty porn: narratives and images of squalor and neglect created for the purpose of immediate, emotional arousal. Like sexual porn, a sense of superiority in the viewer/voyeur is also often elicited, even if unintentionally. Whether for entertainment or in service to serious journalism, Appalachia is regularly portrayed with a kind of sentimental contempt. (All pornography, Flannery O'Connor once noted, is a form of sentimentality: shortcut and indulgence – a foreclosing on complexity and a pleasure-taking in feeling for feeling's sake.)

What is contemptible – even if it is pitied – can never be grievable. People and place collapse in the imagination of the appalled, self-satisfied outsider. When the matter of climate trauma emerges, the poverty frame has already done its work: excluding so much (as all frames do, of course) in the creation of a portrait that occludes recognition of shared vulnerability. Yet the exploitation of Appalachians for the amusement or curiosity of outsiders exists on a continuum with the exploitation of landscapes here and elsewhere that threatens places and people everywhere. Logging, acid mine drainage, mountaintop removal, fracking, gutted economies and wrecked families are some of the causes and casualties of climate trauma in Appalachia. Their invisibility or seeming inevitability presses the question of which ruined places and whose ruined lives are worthy of mourning.

---

3 Butler, *Frames of War*, p. 15.

Changing the frame

The Catholic Committee of Appalachia (CCA) was formed 50 years ago 'to serve Appalachia, her poor and the entire web of creation'.[4] Its original members and allies were committed to Vatican II's vision of the Church as the entire 'People of God' and to the social teaching issued at the end of the Council, which emphasized the dignity of the human person, economic justice, the rights of workers and the role of the Church in listening to the voices of the marginalized. Drawing inspiration from Dorothy Day and others, the CCA has sought to reclaim the Church of the poor and to work alongside those who struggle for redress, whether the injustice is racism, for-profit prisons, or denied access to clean water. In three 'Appalachian Pastorals' – powerfully prophetic letters written in 1975, 1995 and 2015 to clergy, laity and 'all people of goodwill' – the CCA has spoken boldly and gracefully about justice and healing for all of creation. The first two letters were composed collaboratively and endorsed by the bishops of the region. The third letter, 'The Telling Takes Us Home', is designated a 'People's Pastoral', since by 2015 there were no bishops in the 25 dioceses of Appalachia willing to be associated with it. (This is but one sign of how church, national and local politics have changed dramatically in southern Appalachia in the last three decades.) All three letters reflect the CCA's commitment

> to listen to the voices of the people, especially the cry of the poor; to give witness to the cost of humanity's destructive relationship with Earth for both local communities and the planet as a whole; [and] to speak a prophetic word on behalf of a struggling human and wider Earth community.[5]

Before writing the third pastoral, the women religious, lay persons and priests committed to its crafting were determined

---

4 See www.ccappal.org/, accessed 20/05/20.
5 Catholic Committee of Appalachia, 2015, *The Telling Takes Us Home: Taking Our Place in the Stories that Shape Us. A People's Pastoral from the Catholic Committee of Appalachia*, Spencer, WV: Catholic Committee of Appalachia, p. 7.

to listen to the voices of under-represented communities and to ask these persons a single, simple, yet profound question: what is it like to be you in this place? Responses to this question, and the stories that flowed from the conversations it generated, came from residents of mountain communities, coal miners, the homeless, the young, people of colour, Native persons, Latinas and Latinos, LGBTQ persons, sex workers, members of diverse religious communities, people who have left the Catholic Church, and people who have left the region. The voiced experiences challenged reductive narratives about Appalachians so often offered up for public consumption. Conversations with people of colour, for instance, revealed how the 'whiteness' of the region has long been taken for granted, obscuring racial diversity and silencing the stories of persons in non-majority communities. Similarly, Native people noted feeling invisible, in part because indigenous communities are often talked about as if they existed only in the past.

The People's Pastoral also gives voice to the land, to earth's anguish in this place: 'The story of Appalachia is the story of what many call a "sacrifice zone," one of the many places exploited for the sake of a global capitalist economy that seeks the "maximization of profit" at any cost.'[6] The criminal acts of brutality that have destroyed so much here have not been perpetrated on 'the environment' – that sterile, linguistic construct which reveals how alienated many of us are from particular places in the natural world. Rather, what has been violated, in many cases beyond repair or recovery, are known and loved rivers, ridges, creeks, lakes, lanes, mountains, meadows, hills, hollers, towns, cities, creatures and human beings. Perhaps the violence of mountaintop removal is the most shocking, since the force of the explosives used in this kind of mining can crack the foundations of houses and drinking wells near and far. It can cause mudslides and catastrophic flooding. It produces 'flyrock' – fragmented stone, ranging from fine dust to pebbles to boulders – which has been deadly to ecosystems and people. The processes in mountaintop removal destroy topsoil a century in the making and permit rubble dumping in nearby valleys

---

6 Catholic Committee of Appalachia, *The Telling Takes Us Home*, p. 25.

where the headwaters of streams and rivers lie. Exposed rock leaches heavy metals and other toxins that pose enormous health risks to plants, people and other animals. Since the inception of mountaintop removal in the 1970s, the population of cerulean warblers has decreased by 70 per cent and an entire order of mayfly has disappeared from streams below valley fills.[7] The monstrous scars left by the massive, thunderous blasts resemble desolate moonscapes,

> dead zones on our planet which cannot be restored to their prior life-giving condition in our lifetimes. Many people who see these wounds up close lament: 'This land is deader than dead can be,' and 'This is what the end of the world looks like to me.'[8]

Such destruction and death cannot be grieved if the precarity of a place and its people is not perceived, and if precariousness is not recognized as a universally shared creaturely condition. But what if it can be? Might climate catastrophes in other parts of the world awaken us all to the vulnerabilities in all living beings? Can the laments of others in their own wounded places make real the tragedies that can befall anyone in any place? If people across all sorts of divides can perceive the world through the frame of our mutual precarity and learn to grieve all losses, such grief need not lead individually or collectively to despondency. If the world is indeed dying in places like Appalachia and the Amazon rainforest and the Arctic permafrost, we can grieve together and witness to our common hope. Not hope as optimism that everything will be fine but, as Vaclav Havel puts it, hope as an orientation of the spirit: we work for something not because it will succeed but because it is good. This kind of hope is 'the certainty that something makes sense, regardless of how it turns out'.[9]

---

7 See https://appvoices.org/end-mountaintop-removal/ecology/, accessed 20/05/20.

8 Catholic Committee of Appalachia, *The Telling Takes Us Home*, p. 12.

9 Vaclav Havel, 1991, *Disturbing the Peace*, New York: Vintage Books, p. 181.

Palliative care for dying places

In medicine, palliative care can begin at diagnosis and be delivered concurrently with treatments and therapies. Clear-eyed about death, it is committed to helping create the conditions for a good end. For dying places on the planet, what does preparing for death – imminent death and death several generations away – look like? Perhaps a palliative approach to the death and dying brought on by climate trauma invites us to tarry with grief, to remain, as Butler advises, 'exposed to its unbearability', resistant to that smothering cultural pressure to seek closure, and willing instead to honour the pain that living with the dying brings. Tending to someone or something near death and lingering with both the sorrow and satisfaction it can bring is to discover the grief work elemental to the human condition, the grief work that makes us human. And maybe this can return us 'to our collective responsibility for the physical lives of one another'.[10]

A palliative care model for climate death can also transform private pain into communal mourning. Rituals like grief circles and liturgies of lament emerge as necessities in all end-of-life situations. To collectively mourn a lost species or a dying stream is an act of hope: not because it will undo the tragedy but because it is deeply good to mark the tragedy, to name and witness it. Moreover, just as palliative medicine may continue treatments and therapies for a patient, it is important to continue to organize, march, protest and resist – to engage in activism for the sake of our imperilled planet. Collectively sacralizing the sorrow of so much death and dying accompanies this necessary work.

Finally, a palliative care approach to a dying world can help us recover the beautiful – in ourselves, in other beings, in the act of grieving itself. When a person we love is dying, we long to share beauty with them: to have them glimpse their own, to experience it in those who care for them. Facing mortality truthfully – grieving with hope – has a way of making evident and palpable a philosophical truism: part of what it means to *be* is to be beautiful; beauty is not an add-on, it is constitutive of a thing's

---

10 Butler, *Precarious Life*, p. 30.

existence. To face climate death truthfully – to grieve with hope, responsibility and integrity – is to perceive the destruction of the natural world and its inhabitants as a wilful negating of being, thwarting that which makes a threatened arctic ice shelf or the endangered Cheat Mountain salamander what it is. It confronts humanity's apostasy from its own beauty and recognizes that we have abandoned our vocation (*kalos* = beauty, calling) to be caretakers in kinship with all of creation. This pain can also be made sacred as we learn that we belong to the world and one another, all of us companions in grief and hope for the time we have left.

34

The Sinking of the Island

ANUPAMA RANAWANA

Every year, the island was a little less. 'Look,' my father would tell us, distracting our teenage minds from bathing in rock pools, 'Can you see where the waves reach? One day, all of this will sink beneath the sea.' Standing in front of the ocean as a child, then a teenager and then an adult, I was always possessed of the feeling of potent destruction contained in the waves, of the enormity of that which is to come.

> Destruction dances on the vast ocean waves – A fearful festival!
> Beating its hundred wings the storm wind raves in furious squall.
> Ocean and sky conjoin – fierce intercourse …
> Unseeing, unhearing, frenzied giants come,
> Homeless, loveless forms:
> Where do they rush to die, bursting all bonds?[1]

To the cosmos we belong, and to the cosmos will we return, for even the island that gives us nourishment and life must submit to this rule. This was the first theological lesson I ever received.

And so, every time I have returned to the island, I have looked for how it is, always, a little less. With the rising seas and temperatures, I now stand on the beach, look out on to the frothy waves and think of how, someday, both I and this island will disappear. This disappearance – not mine, but the island's – is resisted of course. Countless policy studies, doctoral dissertations and national action plans point out the impact of climate change

---

1 Rabindranath Tagore, 2004, *Selected Poems*, New Delhi: Oxford University Press, p. 7.

on sea-level rise, the damage to coastal communities, their live-lihoods and coastal ecosystems. According to a study by the Universities of Kyoto and Peradeniya, the projected sea-level rise (SLR) in Sri Lanka was 0.3 metres by 2010 and 1.0 metres by 2070. Scientists worryingly note the rate of coastline recession and warn against the damages wrought by pollution and river mining. Further worries have been raised by the building of a Port City on land reclaimed by the sea. The impact of this is already felt. Each year the island feels hotter and hotter.

This moment, now urged on by human folly, will come too soon. There was a moment when it did come, when a tsunami overpowered the island. It left its scars of danger and submission.

> They had been born and grew up in the environment of the sea and the sea coast. The sea was part of their lives, their very selves. They adored and respected the sea in spiritual terms, looking at it as a god, as their mother ... When it arose to strike them down, their families, communities and all their belongings in seconds, the destruction was immense.[2]

I think about this as another – an unnatural and unmoving – wave overpowers the beach from the land side, erasing the sand with scraps of paper, plastic, bottles, lunch packets, rubber and glass. I take a boat ride out to the mangroves near the town I am visiting. These ancient mangroves are legally protected due to their carbon-storing 'superpowers', and for the lives that thrive within their stilt-like roots – fish, prawns, crabs and other marine animals. After the impact of the Boxing Day tsunami of 2004, Sri Lanka became the first country to protect all its mangrove forests. As our boat travels through, I see monkeys, herons, gulls, even a monitor lizard. But emerging from within the mangrove and into the marina, I am distracted by the brightly coloured skirt around the edges of it. On a closer look, it is the imprint of another animal, of the debris of lunch parties, lazy days by the beach, of holidays. I point to it and ask the boatman, 'What is this? This is protected. Doesn't the [council] clean it?'

---

2 D. Somasundaram, 2014, *Scarred Communities: Psychological Impact of Man-Made and Natural Disasters on Sri Lankan Society*, New Delhi: Sage, p. 144.

'Yes, yes, weekly, sometimes monthly. But the waste from the beaches is pulled out with the tide, it gathers at the roots and stays there. You have to stop the litter on the beach.' All at once I see the island sinking under a wave of detritus, a swell of brightly coloured papers festooned with a plethora of names: Nestle, Pepsi, Coca-Cola, Heinz, Parle-G, Carlsberg, Keels, Cargill's, Cadbury, Bisleri, Olu.

But the waves of artificial debris call to mind also the waves of blood, for this island has also faced death in so many ways. There are times when I have wondered if the entire landscape is built on and rebuilds in blood. The island has battled conquerors, invaders, whether they be from neighbouring shores or faraway places where the people 'drank blood and ate stones'. There are names of places that echo this history: '*Kadugannawa*' – the place where the sword was drawn; '*Leyvalle*' – the valley of blood.

> I quickly learned the art:
> chucking English carcases
> off my back.[3]

When the colonizers left, in the wake of their violence, there was insurrection, social uprisings of youth and the marginalized, an exodus of oppressed groups, ethnic tension, civil war, anti-Muslim violence, anti-Tamil violence, anti-Christian violence. We grew up knowing about the young men and women killed by governments, by the LTTE. We grew up with checkpoints on our way to school and shrugging off the news of a bomb if only three people had been killed. In the year of my First Communion, a bomb blew apart the then President. The month before I visited the mangroves and the beach, a bomb had killed 200 people in a local church. Miles away, mothers and grandmothers have sat in protest for 300 days, demanding to know the stories of their children, now lost in a war.

What, then, is theology for an island with its histories of blood and dying, for an island where rising seas mean other, perhaps more furious, deaths, where the beaches choke with plastic and

---

3 Romesh Gunasekera, 1989, 'Two Poems', *London Review of Books* 11(4), 16 February.

paper and glass, where manufactured port cities add to rising heat?

Michael Northcott has argued that we may use traditional rituals from our faith communities that can shape approaches to climate justice, particularly the actions of pilgrimage, sanctuary and Eucharist.[4] To this, I venture to add that of ritual mourning, of weeping. When I consider the answer to the question above, it is a rending and tearing of garments that comes to mind. There is a need, here and globally, perhaps, for a theology of weeping, or for weeping to form the focus of our prayers. *Is weeping a form of prayer?* A few years ago, in thinking about the Eurocentrism of theology, I wondered about weeping as a decolonizing action.[5] In grief and in mourning we become unsettled and begin to rethink the world as we know it. As Du Bois has noted, we need to stop being 'fence sitters'. In any experience of grief, there arises a 'soul-torn strength' that can push us to ask uncomfortable questions, do uncomfortable things. A decolonial rendering, as scholars like Quijano, Grosfugeul, Dussel, Ndlovu-Gatsheni and Rutazibwa have noted, is to encourage systemic and historical analysis of the organized (re)production of injustice and mass human suffering. The process of individual and collective grieving can trigger such analysis.

> Bewildered we are and passion tossed, mad with the madness of mobbed and mocked and murdered people: straining at the armposts of Thy throne … what meaneth this? Tell us the plan: give us the sign![6]

Once again, as I think about theology for/of/within/about dying, I can only form thoughts of weeping. There is a need to weep together, to weep in solidarity, for the destruction and the death

---

4 M. Northcott, 2013, *A Political Theology of Climate Change*, Grand Rapids, MI: Eerdmans.

5 Anupama Ranawana, 2016, 'In Weeping We Begin to Decolonize Our Theologies', *Political Theology Network*, 30 July, https://politicaltheology.com/in-weeping-we-begin-to-decolonize-our-theologies-anupama-ranwana/, accessed 18/08/2020.

6 *Du Bois, W. E. B. (William Edward Burghardt), 1868–1963. Litany of Atlanta: A, 1906. W. E. B. Du Bois Papers (MS 312).* Special Collections and University Archives, University of Massachusetts Amherst Libraries.

that has occurred throughout the island's, as well as global, history. We can also weep in anticipation, for the island that will sink, for deaths that have been and are to come. In allowing for this lamentation, we can allow ourselves to heal, but, more importantly, we are forced into considering what is necessary for collective healing, and redemption in the here and now. If I cry over the choked roots of the mangrove tree, I become more conscious of my ecological sin and am moved to repentance, to working towards a transformed world. The theologian Aloy Peiris[7] and the activist and preacher Sojourner Truth[8] – among others – would both point us towards this from their different Christian traditions. Here, we are charged not to focus solely on an other-worldly conception of the afterlife, but to see virtue and purpose demanding justice now. To be religious in this instance is inseparable from an exhortation to construct a truly democratic existence.[9] Perhaps the best example of this is Dorothy Day, who, moved by her own experience of the wretchedness of the world and her understanding of the salvific nature of the cross, worked to build a vision of community and hospitality – a third way between submission and violent revolution.[10] Theologies that reflect on a dying world must harvest the energy of sorrow and grief to engender a spiritual revolution. It must enter the passion and energy of the people, and through this recognize and remember a God who breaks the chains of slavery, who will break the binds of destruction.

I consider images of the Madonna weeping as she ponders the fate of her Son, who sacrifices himself for the world. The Madonna – whom Tissa Balasuriya, a Roman Catholic priest and activist from Sri Lanka, pointed us towards, for he saw the action of the Church in the world as an extension of Mary's

---

7 A. Peiris, 1988, *An Asian Theology of Liberation*, MaryKnoll, NY: Orbis Books.

8 Isabelle K. Richman, 2016, *Sojourner Truth: A Prophet of Social Justice*, New York: Routledge.

9 Jonathon S. Kahn, 2009, *The Religious Imagination of W. E. B. Du Bois*, Oxford: Oxford University Press.

10 S. Marsh, 2012, '"The Odds and Ends of Things": Dorothy Day's 1930s Catholic Worker Columns and the Prudent Translation of Catholic Social Teachings', *Rhetoric Society Quarterly* 42(4), pp. 330–52.

concern: she is 'the disciple who works for that justice which sets free the oppressed and for that charity which assists the needy; but, above all, the disciple who is the active witness of that love which builds up Christ in people's hearts'.[11] As the Madonna weeps, we are all invited to weep. We must take on the anguish of this social death, weeping for what has happened and our own complicity in fostering this reality.

When on the cross, the Son experienced all the anguish of the world, and because of this we are now invited into God's presence. Experienced in our sorrow, the Divine understands our despair. Surely, in order to enter into God's presence, and to make his grace visible, we too are called to weep in despair. While grief and despair are symbiotic states, what allows us to express feelings of despair, without giving in to it, could be the work of transformative justice. Yohanna Katanacho has also spoken of weeping and crying together in order to confront catastrophic realities.

> This is a season of weeping and mourning, but it is not void of hope.
> Our tears are the bridge between brutality and humanity.
> Our tears are the salty gates for seeing a different reality.[12]

Such weeping moves us to repentance for ecological and historical sins. In 2011, at a meeting in Quito, Anglican bishops referred to the mounting urgency of the environmental crisis and noted that central to this was sorrow and repentance. Pope Francis has urged a 'theology of tears' as the only true response to the question of why the innocent (and, in this instance, shall we say the earth is the innocent) suffers. Mourning and repentance may urge the necessary spiritual awakening that must be centred now. This is the spiritual, intellectual and emotional dimension of land – the knowledge of co-existence with rivers, streams, air, wind. A

---

11 T. Balasuriya, 1997, *Mary and Human Liberation*, Harrisburg, PA: Trinity Press International.

12 Yohanna Katanacho, 2017, 'A Theology of Tears: Cry with Us', *IFES*, https://ifesworld.org/en/journal/a-theology-of-tears-cry-with-us/, accessed 29/05/20.

spiritual awakening is necessary to address the global ecological crisis. These awakenings lead us to consider the true meaning of inter-being within creation.[13] What do we see through our tears?

When this exists, that comes to be; with the arising of this, that arises. When this does not exist, that does not come to be; with the cessation of this, that ceases.[14]

Further Reading

E. Dussel, 1993, 'Eurocentrism and Modernity (Introduction to the Frankfurt Lectures)', *Boundary 2* 20(3), pp. 65–76.

R. Grosfoguel and A. M. Cervantes-Rodriguez, 2002, 'Introduction: Unthinking Twentieth-century Eurocentric Mythologies: Universal Knowledge, Decolonization, and Developmentalism' in R. Grosfoguel and A. M. Cervantes-Rodriguez (eds), *The Modern/Colonial/Capitalist World-System in the Twentieth Century: Global Processes, Antisystemic Movements, and the Geopolitics of Knowledge*, Westport, CT: Praeger Publishers.

S. J. Ndlovu-Gatsheni, 2012, 'Coloniality of Power in Development Studies and the Impact of Global Imperial Designs on Africa', *Australasian Review of African Studies* 33(2), pp. 48–73.

A. Quijano, 2007, 'Coloniality and Modernity/Rationality', *Cultural Studies* 21(2–3), pp. 168–78.

O. U. Rutazibwa, 2018, 'On Babies and Bathwater: Decolonizing International Development Studies' in S. de Jong, R. Icaza and O. U. Rutazibwa (eds), *Decolonization and Feminisms in Global Teaching and Learning*, London: Routledge, pp. 192–214.

---

13 L. M. Ling, 2017, 'World Politics in Colour', *Millennium, Journal of International Studies* 45(3), pp. 473–91.

14 A. Ranawana and J. Trafford, 2019, 'Imperialist Environmentalism and Decolonial Struggle', *Discover Society*, https://discoversociety.org/2019/08/07/imperialist-environmentalism-and-decolonial-struggle/, accessed 29/05/20.

35

Tree

AZARIAH FRANCE-WILLIAMS

If the world ended tomorrow, I would still plant one tree
betrothed to beloved earth, as I bend on one knee
Before I say I love you, I offer my apology
I commit to you.
I pray you won't abandon me.

Conclusion:
World Without End

Glory to the Father
And to the Son
And to the Holy Ghost
As it was in the beginning
is now
and ever shall be
world without end.

Whenever I express my love for the phrase 'world without end', someone will take it upon themselves to remind me that the *original Latin* is actually *saecula saeculorum*, which means ages of ages, or for ever, and is *not the same* as saying that *this world* has *no end*. That is fine, I say, but if God will be given glory from the beginning and is given glory now, then this future for ever, world without end, ages unto ages somehow exists in relation with these other points in space-time. Creation, the incarnation, death, and resurrection of Christ – all these holy, *earthy* events – are also God's eternal glory. At the end of a book about death I want to talk about resurrection, and not just my own, but the resurrection of all things. This is not because I think resurrection provides a get-out card for grief, or even necessarily a daily balm, but because I want to understand what grieving the earth means if I also believe that the earth will be resurrected.

Of course, many Christians maintain that Jesus' resurrection says nothing about earthly resurrection, and nor do they imagine that our resurrected selves will be anything like humans as we are now. And maybe the promise of ongoing, resurrected existence *could* be riven from the gifts of finite space, of touch, of being a body (I think this summarizes the way many imagine heaven). But I do not take comfort in the thought of myself cruelly extracted from the sweet blessing of being flesh among flesh, discarding the songs of praise offered by so many beloved creatures for millennia upon millennia. I do not think this is the promise of the Word who was made flesh, dwelt and died among us, was alive again, and ascended to the Father *with body*. Body without end! Do we realize what we say in the creeds? This resurrected man who touched, and was scarred, and ate, was the man who was born of a woman, made of the dust of the Earth, and dwells at the heart of God, ages unto ages, for ever. Our grief over the world is not misplaced affection for temporary shelter. Instead, it recognizes the gift of a home so deeply loved that the giver would join it, take on its nature, and commit to bearing it for ever.

I am not suggesting that grieving a dying world as a Christian is all that different to the grief of someone who does not believe our destruction will be redeemed. We share common griefs, even though our experiences are shaped by the particular places to which we belong. Grief is, for all of us, a means of survival – a healthy way to deal with immense suffering. It prevents us from becoming bitter, or closed off, or indifferent. Grief, especially when shared with others, can make us more generous, tender people. And I think we grieve in order to be honest about how things are, and how we are. So much of the death around us springs from gainful dishonesty; dishonesty about the sanctity of each creature, dishonesty about the likely consequences of our actions, and covering up those consequences when they happen. If we cannot bring ourselves to be truthful about our broken histories, or the current trauma we face and perpetuate, we cannot begin to heal.

Survival, compassion, honesty. These are all good reasons to grieve. But the conviction that Christ's resurrection marked the death of death also contains the hope that our works of love in the present are not consigned to destruction. They participate in a transformed future. As this book took shape I became increasingly convinced that grief is not only a response to losing something loved, or a motivator for behaving in loving ways, but a work of love itself. I have found myself wanting to put words to something that feels so mysterious as to be unspeakable – that our grief over a dying world is more than compassion or repentance. It is also a work that transforms us and the world around us. As love, our grief is shaped but not constrained by the places and time we are given. It is able to stretch beyond our own worlds, our own self-help mantras, our own comforts, even into the ages of ages.

Prophecies, tongues and knowledge will all come to an end. But *love never ends*. It is not that our expressions of love are full or healed: 'now we see through a glass, darkly; but then face to face' (1 Corinthians 13.12, KJV). But nevertheless, our grief, like the world it loves, is not wasted. Reading these stories of grief and courage – of *love* – has been a dark glass through which I anticipate the One and the world I long to see face to face. It is humbling to begin with those things that are lost and broken as my blurred window for truth about the world. But if the body of Christ is a place where I can learn to look through the glass, then that is what I am trying to do, knowing I do not look alone. The world is not indifferent to pain, and nor is the One who made it, and who will make it whole. These pages gather our shared longing to describe this grief, reveal the love that burns at its heart, and offer the courage to pursue it.

I do not intend to sanctify trauma or treat suffering as necessary for love. But we are currently unable to love the world without being willing to expose ourselves to the pain of its death. And grief contains power; if we do not learn how to grieve as a work of love, we will continue to hurt one another. I have coexisted for a long time with the kind of crushing sadness which compels me to worship at the altar of my own despair, feeding hungrily on tears for their own sake, offering up sorrow which does not love life so much as it loves its own abyss. I know the consequences of grieving badly, and I know that I am still trying to learn to grieve well. Becoming open to the grief of others rather than imagining I grieve alone turns me out of myself. It is teaching me to practise the kind of grief which sings that the world is both dying and being made, and made over again, by love.

Thank you for reading with me. The world that love makes is a world without end. Look through the glass darkly. And be assured that our grief will not be wasted.

A Benediction

Sorrows may surround you,
Sadness overwhelm you,
Yet be confident of this:
that you shall see the goodness of the Lord
in the land of the living.
And now may this God,
who holds you in trouble, tends you in sorrow,
and leads you to green pastures,
This three-in-one and one-in-three God,
Bless you, and bless you, and bless you.

Maggi Dawn

Acknowledgements

Responsibility for this book falls with David Shervington, who first invited me to write for SCM Press following the inaugural Theology Slam in 2019. He believed I could produce a book before I did and willingly supported this project when it was still an idea on an A4 page, with no guarantee of any other contributors offering their work. I am so grateful for his constant enthusiasm and encouragement.

The book would have been impossible without the many individuals and organizations who willingly passed on the call for pitches and made sure it fell into the right hands. There are too many to name here, but I would like particularly to thank multiple staff at Tearfund, Wendy Lloyd (Christian Aid), Rachel Carnegie (the Anglican Alliance), Rebecca Boardman (USPG), Andrew Tomlinson (the Church of Scotland), Megan Bedford-Strohm, Daniel Castillo, Rachel Mash, the Society of St Francis, Matthew Humphrey (A Rocha Canada) and John Cooper (Fellowship of Reconciliation). I am also sure that I am indebted to many others who passed on the project's details without me knowing, or who I have forgotten to mention. If that is you, thank you.

Editing a collection is an exercise in giving up control. It turns out that I am bad at this. Thank you to Caleb, the most consistently patient spouse and writing companion I could ask for. He has calmly challenged my anxiety at every stage of this process, and he is always willing to tell me which of my sentences are bad ones.

Finally, and most importantly, thank you to everyone who offered a contribution to this collection, whether you are featured here or not. Your stories will change the Church. Keep telling them.

Acknowledgement of Scripture Quotations